PSALMS

BRINGING THE BIBLE TO LIFE

Genesis, by John H. Walton, Janet Nygren, and Karen H. Jobes
(12 sessions)

Esther, by Karen H. Jobes and Janet Nygren
(8 sessions)

Psalms, by Gerald Wilson, Janet Nygren, and Karen H. Jobes
(10 sessions)

Daniel, by Tremper Longman III, Janet Nygren, and Karen H. Jobes
(10 sessions)

Mark, by David E. Garland, Karen-Lee Thorp, and Karen H. Jobes
(12 sessions)

John, by Gary M. Burge, Karen Lee-Thorp, and Karen H. Jobes
(12 sessions)

Acts, by Ajith Fernando, Karen Lee-Thorp, and Karen H. Jobes
(12 sessions)

Romans, by Douglas J. Moo, Karen Lee-Thorp, and Karen H. Jobes
(12 sessions)

Galatians, by Scot McKnight, Karen Lee-Thorp, and Karen H. Jobes
(6 sessions)

Ephesians, by Klyne Snodgrass, Karen Lee-Thorp, and Karen H. Jobes
(6 sessions)

Hebrews, by George H. Guthrie, Janet Nygren, and Karen H. Jobes
(8 sessions)

Revelation, by Craig S. Keener, Janet Nygren, and Karen H. Jobes
(10 sessions)

BRINGING
THE
BIBLE
TO LIFE

PSALMS

The Cries of the Faithful

Gerald H. Wilson
and Janet Nygren

Karen H. Jobes, Series Editor

ZONDERVAN.com/
AUTHORTRACKER
follow your favorite authors

ZONDERVAN

Psalms
Copyright © 2010 by Gerald H. Wilson, Janet Nygren, and Karen H. Jobes

Requests for information should be addressed to:

Zondervan, *Grand Rapids, Michigan 49530*

ISBN 978-0-310-32437-9

Cover design: Tammy Johnson
Cover photography: Fotosearch, Superstock
Interior design: Michelle Espinoza

Printed in the United States of America

10 11 12 13 14 15 16 /DCI/ 25 24 23 22 21 20 19 18 17 16 15 14 13 12 11 10 9 8 7 6 5 4 3 2 1

CONTENTS

SERIES PREFACE

Have you ever been in a small-group Bible study where the leader read a passage from the Bible and then invited the members of the group to share what the passage meant to them? God wants to speak to each person individually through the Bible, but such an approach to a group study can often be a frustrating and shallow experience for both leader and participants. And while the same passage can speak in various ways into people's lives, the meat of the Word is found in what the biblical writer intended to say about God and our relationship to him. The Bringing the Bible to Life series is for those who are ready to move from a surface reading of the Bible into a deeper understanding of God's Word.

But the Bible, though perhaps familiar, was written in ancient languages and in times quite different from our own, so most readers need a bit more help getting to a deeper understanding of its message. A study that begins and ends with what a passage "means to me" leaves the meaning of the passage unanchored and adrift in the thoughts — and perhaps the misunderstanding — of the reader. But who has time to delve into the history, language, cultures, and theology of the Bible? That's the work of biblical scholars who spend their lives researching, teaching, and writing about the ancient Scriptures. The need is to get the fruit of all that research into the hands of those in small-group Bible studies.

Zondervan's NIV Application Commentary series was written to bring the best of evangelical biblical scholarship to those who want to know *both* the historical meaning of the biblical text *and* its contemporary significance. This companion series, Bringing the Bible to Life, is intended to bring that material into small-group studies in an easy-to-use format. Pastors, Christian education teachers, and small-group leaders whether in church, campus, or home settings will find these guides to be an enriching resource.

Each guide in the series provides an introduction to the biblical book that concisely summarizes the background information needed to better understand the original historical context. Six to twelve sessions per guide, with each session consisting of ten to twelve discussion questions, allow a focused study that moves beyond superficial Bible reading. Relevant excerpts from the corresponding NIVAC commentary provide easy access into additional material for those interested in going even deeper. A closing section in each session assists the group in responding to God's Word together or individually. Guidance for leading each session is included, making the task of small-group leadership more manageable for busy lives.

If you want to move from the biblical text to contemporary life on solid ground, this series has been written for you.

Karen H. Jobes, PhD
Gerald F. Hawthorne Professor of
New Testament Greek and Exegesis
Wheaton College and Graduate School

OF SPECIAL NOTE

Your experience with and understanding of the Psalms can be deepened and enriched by referring to the volume on which it is based: *The NIV Application Commentary: Psalms, Vol. 1*, by Gerald H. Wilson, published by Zondervan in 2002.

INTRODUCTION[1]

Where do you begin a study of Psalms? If you're anything like me, you know they're a rich treasure, but it's a little tricky knowing where to jump in. Some of them sound very similar. Some of them are hard to understand, or seem outdated. Some of them don't relate to your current situation at all. And when you really want help expressing yourself to God through the psalms, how do you find the one you're looking for? This study guide isn't going to be able to answer all your questions. It will take a lifetime to plumb the depths of the psalms, and then some! But I hope it will help to give you a start.

Trying to cover even the first 72 of the 150 psalms is admittedly a challenge. Most groups are not prepared to commit to the time it would take to study every psalm in depth. So I have divided the sessions into categories based on types of psalms. Each lesson covers four psalms, giving you the cumulative flavor of what that type of psalm offers. I found that studying them together revealed a richness that I would have missed looking at them individually. Each session also gives a list of other psalms of that type so that you can look at them further, or have a resource for looking up the type of psalm you're interested in at any particular time. Structuring the study guide this way misses out on what can be learned by reading the psalms in the order they were assembled. However, my hope is that the tools you learn by studying psalm types will enable you to look at all of them in order in greater depth on your own.

Most of the psalms in Psalms 1–72 are attributed to ancient Israel's King David. But they were most likely collected together and arranged during the exile and later. For many of the psalms, that meant they were understood and used differently by those who assembled them than when they were first written, because of the intervening history — nearly a thousand years in some cases. Many see Psalms 1–41 (Book I) as psalms that celebrated David's kingship in Israel. But then the exile took place. Human kingship didn't seem quite as grand from the perspective of people living far away from the Promised Land under a foreign king. Many of the promises in the psalms began to be reinterpreted as messianic — promising future hope to Israel for a time when God reestablished his kingdom. Much of Psalms 42–72 (Book II) can be understood this way. Because we live in a time after the promised Messiah has come, the psalms can be understood in a yet different light, and the New Testament authors help us to make some of those leaps in understanding because we can see how they understood the psalm in relation to Jesus Christ. Keep these things in mind as you read the psalms.

Another change we see from the time the psalms were originally written is a switch from communal to individual use. We believe many psalms were originally composed for communal worship, especially given the notations in the headings. But they are seldom used that way now. This shift probably took place long ago, when worship in the temple was no longer possible — first because of the exile, and later because it was permanently destroyed. But the psalms remain with us as God's Word speaking into our lives, guiding us in personal prayer, and providing a resource for worship through liturgy and singing.

Throughout the study guide I will introduce some tips on how to look at Hebrew poetry for better understanding, but a few introductory comments are in order. The conventions that define poetry vary from language to language. In the Hebrew language there is much less emphasis on rhyme and meter than there is in English poetry. What is more important in Hebrew poetry is parallelism and structure. Parallelism comes in different forms, but basically looks at adjacent lines and how they build on each other, or how they make a point through contrasts. Repetition of words or their synonyms are important to note, as well as the overall structure of a psalm — particularly the beginning, middle, and end stanzas.

With that said, I invite you to open your heart and delve into your study of the psalms, learning from the psalmist what it means to cry out to God whatever your circumstance.

NOTE

1. This introduction is based on *The NIV Application Commentary: Psalms, Vol. 1* (hereafter referred to as *NIVAC: Psalms, Vol. 1*) by Gerald Wilson (Grand Rapids: Zondervan, 2002), 19–81.

THE PSALMS
AS WISDOM

Psalms 1, 19, 25, 37[1]

O ne of my favorite children's books is *Petunia*.[2] In the story, Petunia the silly goose believes she has become wise just because she finds a book. After causing all sorts of trouble in the farmyard, she realizes in the end that it's not enough to carry wisdom under her wing. She must put it in her mind and in her heart. Dare I suggest that we often imitate this silly goose ourselves? God has given us an abundance of instruction and wisdom in the psalms, yet we often act on what we think we know is contained in them, while foolishly stumbling around, causing trouble for ourselves and others. I invite you to open the book and begin to drink deeply of the wisdom contained within.

THE WISDOM PSALMS CONTRAST
DIFFERENT WAYS OF LIFE[3]

Read Psalm 1.

This first psalm has often been understood as an introduction to all the other psalms; in fact, in earlier manuscripts it wasn't even numbered so that it would be seen that way.[4] So it's fitting that Psalm 1 would give us clues as to how to study the rest of Psalms, and appropriate that it be classified as a wisdom psalm — one that teaches us how to look at life.

1. How would you define "the law of the LORD" (1:2)? Would it include the psalms? According to 1:2, how should we view the law of the LORD? "Day and night" (v. 2) is a *merism*, a poetic tool that describes two extremes which really includes everything in between as well.[5] What would meditating on God's law day and night look like in real life?

2. Psalm 1 describes two distinctly different ways to live life. What are the blessings of living the righteous life (1:3, 6a)? Compare this description with Jeremiah 17:7 – 8. What does Jeremiah add to your understanding? Compare both descriptions to Revelation 22:1 – 2. How does this complete the picture of abundant life?

3. What are the consequences for living life according to any way other than God's law (1:4 – 5, 6b)? How did Jesus view people who lived this way (see Luke 5:27 – 31; 11:39 – 54)? How does your life line up?

The psalm is, then, an exhortation—through positive and negative examples—to adopt the fruitful and satisfying life characterized by immersion in God. Then and only then will the faithful find themselves on the "way" that is blazed and watched over by God himself.[6]

THE WISDOM PSALMS CELEBRATE GOD'S LAW[7]

Read Psalm 19.

4. According to 19:1–6 (and from your own experience), what do the heavens tell us about God? How far and how frequently does the message go out? The sun is singled out as a voice representing all the other heavenly voices, a literary device called *metonymy.*[8] If the sun could talk, what would it say about its satisfaction with the role God gave it, according to this psalm?

5. God gave us more than creation to tell us about himself. How does his law (and its synonyms—statutes, precepts, commands, ordinances) communicate to us (19:7–11)? According to 19:7–10, how good are his guidelines? If we were to live according to the way God created us to, following his ways, what benefits would we receive?

His Guidelines Restore the soul.
His law (word) Revives us;
makes us wise.
gives joy to the heart;
gives light to the eyes.
Warns us;
Rewards us.

6. With all God gives us to let us know about himself, and all that he provides for us to know how to live, what's the problem? Why do we struggle so much to live like we believe it (19:12–13)? What two kinds of faults does the psalmist acknowledge? How can we run our course, like the sun in verse 5, to achieve the joy God wants for us (see Heb. 12:1–2)?

Let go, let God.

GOING DEEPER

Humans are not left alone and forlorn with no purpose or meaning in life. God's Word—his Torah—is a delight because through it we discover who God is and how to assume our place within his creation—a place of unexpected honor, responsibility, and communion with him.[9]

THE WISDOM PSALMS HAVE THE INTENT TO TEACH[10]

Read Psalm 25.

7. One poetic feature of some of the wisdom psalms is an acrostic structure, where each line or set of lines starts with succeeding letters of the Hebrew alphabet—virtually impossible to detect in an English translation aside from a footnote.[11] Psalm 25 is one such psalm. How could this poetic device be helpful for instruction? What other clues does the psalm give about its intent to teach (vv. 4–5, 8–9, 12, 14)?

— Guide me in your truth & teach me.
— my hope is in you all day long.
— make me, teach me, lead me

8. What does the psalmist teach us in regard to how he views himself (vv. 7a, 9, 11, 15–18)? The Hebrew word translated "soul" in verse 1 ("To you, O LORD, I lift up my soul" [NIV]) "is much more than mind or soul. It is the essential integrated being that is sustained in life by the animating breath/spirit given by God ... the level of deepest concern."[12] Because of this, some more recent translations read "In you, LORD my God, I put my trust." What can we learn from the psalmist, who lifts up the very essence of his being to God while at the same time being honest about who he is?

humble – listen to God.
God wants us to pursue him.
Faith = believing in him

The life of the psalms is messy life where pain and joy, self-knowledge and self-doubt, love and hatred, trust and suspicion break in upon one another, overlapping and competing for our attention. It is a life in which we have real choices on a daily basis between life and death.... And in these psalms this messy life—this real life—is constantly brought before God as our own messiness ought to be, *before* it is cleaned up and sanitized. God wants us to bring *all* of life before him as the psalmists do rather than just the parts we consider acceptable.[13]

9. What does the psalmist reveal about God that allows him to come before God so honestly? What does it say about his relationship with God? How can your own relationship with God grow similarly?

THE WISDOM PSALMS CONNECT OUR ACTIONS WITH ULTIMATE CONSEQUENCES[14]

Read Psalm 37.

10. As you read this psalm, hopefully you are beginning to pick up on some features that mark it as a wisdom psalm. What characteristics does it share with other psalms we've already looked at? What is the basic problem that it addresses?

11. Like virtually all the psalms in Book I of the Psalms (1–41), this psalm is attributed to David. How does the fact that the psalm is connected to a real person add to the legitimacy of its observations? How does the wisdom of the psalm reflect real-life experience (v. 25)?

12. Based on David's experience and his understanding of God's ways, why should the righteous continue to trust God and persevere in right living in spite of the temptation to pursue other lifestyles?

GOING DEEPER

Often, when confronted by evil in our world without and within, we look to God for escape. When, like the psalmists, we find our circumstances remain unchanged, God can seem distant, absent, and unconcerned.... The great and difficult truth God is teaching us is this: Life in a world thoroughly corrupted by human evil is going to remain difficult and painful! God cannot remove us from the pain of living without removing us from living itself.[15]

RESPONDING TO GOD'S WORD

IN YOUR GROUP:

We often think of Psalms as poetry more than wisdom, but now there's no escaping what you've learned! What other sources of wisdom do you look to for guidance about how to live your life? On a scale of 1 to 10, rate each source on how heavily you rely on it, and then on how reliable you've found it to be. Compare your results.

ON YOUR OWN:

We don't have the benefit of the acrostic structure in English to help us learn, but consider memorizing the beginning of Psalm 25. Set aside time to pray each day and start your time with Psalm 25:1–7. Consider carefully what it means to lift up the very essence of your being during your prayer time.

NOTES

1. Other psalms in this category among Pss. 1–72 include Pss. 14, 34, 49, 52, 53, and 62.
2. Roger Duvoisin, *Petunia* (New York: Alfred A. Knopf, 1950).
3. This section is based on *NIVAC: Psalms, Vol. 1*, 89–105.
4. Wilson, 92.
5. Wilson, 50, 96.
6. Wilson, 93.
7. This section is based on *NIVAC: Psalms, Vol. 1*, 359–380.
8. Wilson, 364.
9. Wilson, 380.
10. This section is based on *NIVAC: Psalms, Vol. 1*, 459–469.
11. Further discussion of acrostic poetry can be found in Wilson, 55–57.
12. Wilson, 451.
13. Wilson, 100–101.
14. This section is based on *NIVAC: Psalms, Vol. 1*, 600–613.
15. Wilson, 613.

EXPRESSIONS OF DAVID'S LIFE

Psalms 52, 57, 63, 18[1]

Revealer → not
A concealer!

I f these psalms merely describe "David's response to a personal circumstance centuries—even millennia—ago, why ought I to assume that [these psalms] can influence the way I respond today to my own situations of distress?"[2] The differences between David's personal circumstances, culture, and role in Israel's history and our own are almost beyond comparison. Yet David was a man after God's own heart (1 Sam. 13:14; 16:7). His life pointed ahead in many ways to Jesus, God's appointed king who reigns forever. As we look at how David reacts to his circumstances, we have before us the example of a righteous—not perfect—man responding in a very personal way to God. But the psalms help us to go far beyond that, to understand the God that David cries out to, trusts, and worships, and our own role in God's kingdom as we face daily challenges.

DAVID'S HOPE WAS IN GOD ALONE[3]

Read Psalm 52.

1. This psalm about a specific incident in David's life fits the characteristics
   of a wisdom psalm, like the ones we studied in the first session. Before
   looking at the historical circumstances, what features do you see in the
   psalm that make it fit in that category?

2. David was anointed king of Israel when it became clear that God rejected
   Saul as king (1 Sam. 15–16), but it was years before he actually took the
   throne. Saul grew to love David, but then was consumed with jealousy and
   sought David's life (1 Sam. 18–19). Saul's agenda became more and more
   his own, not God's, with each step he took. The superscription of Psalm
   52 says it was written "when Doeg the Edomite had gone to Saul and told
   him: 'David has gone to the house of Ahimelek.'" This event happened
   after David fled Saul's household, only to be chased until Saul died. Read
   1 Samuel 21–22 to better understand the context of the psalm. How
   does understanding the occasion that prompted David to write the psalm
   impact your reading of it? Why might Doeg be characterized as an evil
   man by David if he is simply carrying out Saul's orders?

3. The words of David's psalm were true on more levels than even he may
   have realized at the time he wrote them. Ahimelek the priest was a descen-
   dant of Eli, whose sons "were scoundrels; they had no regard for the LORD"
   (1 Sam. 2:12). Read the prophecy for Eli's family in 1 Samuel 2:30–33.
   (Also consider 1 Samuel 21:7; 22:6, 16, 18, 22.) Who was responsible for

the death of the priests and the town? Looking at Psalm 52 again, what evidence do you see that David's psalm applies more generally than he intended? What implications does this have for your own life?

DAVID ACTED ON AN UNDERSTANDING OF GOD'S LOVE AND FAITHFULNESS[4]

Read Psalm 57.

4. Though not specified, Psalm 57 is likely based on events described in 1 Samuel 24, as Saul continued to pursue David around the countryside. Read 1 Samuel 24. How does David call into question the definition of an enemy? What seems to be of greater concern to David than his own safety?

5. Keep thinking about David's primary concern as you look at Psalm 57. What is the theme of the song mentioned in verse 9 that he would like the whole world to know? (Hint: look for repetition throughout the psalm—it usually signifies something important.) How does David display confidence of that message in his own life? In his response to Saul?

This is light breaking forth in the midst of darkness. "The light shines in the darkness, but the darkness has not overcome … it" (John 1:5). Like our own experience of Christ, often God breaks in as light into our own darkness. Darkness may remain before and after, but the light, kindled by the life, death, and work of Jesus, continues to shine in the darkness and not to be overcome. This is a marvelous and encouraging image.[5]

6. David declares, "I cry out to God Most High, to God, who fulfills his purpose for me" (57:2, NIV). For David, that meant God saving his life to be Israel's next king. For Jesus, that meant losing his life for the sake of saving others but being resurrected from the grave. In both, God's glory was shown on earth as a result of fulfilling his purposes in them (see John 17:4). How is God's glory shown as he fulfills his purpose in you? What implications does it have in regard to your circumstances or "enemies"?

DAVID VALUED GOD'S LOVE MORE THAN LIFE ITSELF[6]

Read Psalm 63.

7. Psalm 63 was written "when [David] was in the Desert of Judah" (see superscription), likely in that same time period when Saul was chasing him (1 Sam. 21 – 31).[7] The imagery of a parched traveler looking for water is a powerful one, particularly to someone familiar with travel in a desert environment. How extensive is the psalmist's longing (63:1)? What does it mean to carry this imagery over to a longing for God? How did Jesus use similar imagery in his teaching (John 4:13 – 14; 7:37 – 38)?

8. You can think of thirst as looking at the half-empty part of a glass. How does David know what he's missing (63:2–8)? How does Jesus know that to an even greater degree (John 12:44–46; Heb. 1:1–3)? Where did Jesus experience the same kind of longing as David (John 19:28)?

9. According to Jesus, when we believe in him we should no longer experience this thirst for God because he's given us his Spirit (John 7:38–39). Yet many can probably relate to David's experience of unquenched spiritual thirst. What sort of enemy do we now face that can create the same sense of isolation that David describes in Psalm 63 (see Eph. 6:12)? How can David's psalm become our psalm?

GOING DEEPER

Is there some way here and now that the love of God ... makes that kind of difference in your life? Does it make such a difference that it wouldn't be worth living without it? Is your connection with God so important to you that you would sacrifice all your future hopes and dreams to keep connected with God?... [Jesus] went to the cross willingly because God's love ... was better than life.... May God's committed covenant love so fill you that you will come to know the abundant life that does not depend on our ability to stay alive.[8]

DAVID KNEW GOD AS A
REFUGE IN TIMES OF TROUBLE[9]

Read Psalm 18.

10. This psalm is too long to cover in depth, but we end this session with it because it refers to the Lord's deliverance of David after years of fleeing from Saul. Read 1 Samuel 29 and 31 for the details of Saul's death. After all the years of the chase, what is David's involvement with Saul's end? How does the psalmist's account differ from the description in 1 Samuel? Can they be talking about the same thing? How would you explain the differences?

11. How serious was David's predicament according to the psalmist (18:4–5, 16–17)? Why did God save him (18:6, 19, 25–26, 50)? What's it like to have God on your side (18:7–19)?

12. Being on God's side does not guarantee us safety from our enemies, from persecution, suffering, disasters, etc. (at least in this present earthly existence). But that's not to say that God doesn't equip us with real help for real situations. What kind of help did David receive from God (18:30–45)? How do you see some of that worked out in 1 Samuel 29 and 31? How have you experienced God's help in the circumstances of your own life?

GOING DEEPER

God as "rock," "refuge," and "shield" are not fuzzy, pious, hopeful concepts to the psalmist; they are grounded in the harsh and yet practical context of real-world experience. God here is not a vague, "pie-in-the-sky-by-and-by" future hope but an effective reality of strength and deliverance here and now.[10]

RESPONDING TO GOD'S WORD

IN YOUR GROUP:

The variety of events that resulted in the psalms of this session sprang from different emotions in David—anger, hope, fear, longing, praise, etc. Discuss what situations are most likely to cause you to cry out to God in one way or another. Is there a common thread in your stories, or are they all different?

ON YOUR OWN:

Think of a specific event in your own life when you were very aware of God's presence and help. How would you express it in a psalm of your own?

NOTES

1. Many psalms are attributed to David, but these are connected to specific events in David's life. Other such psalms among Pss. 1–72 include Pss. 3, 34, 51, 54, 56, 59 and 60.
2. Wilson, 128, said of Psalm 3, the first of the psalms tied to a specific event.
3. This section is based on *NIVAC: Psalms, Vol. 1*, 784–790.
4. This section is based on *NIVAC: Psalms, Vol. 1*, 829–838.
5. Wilson, 837.
6. This section is based on *NIVAC: Psalms, Vol. 1*, 888–896.
7. Wilson, 889.
8. Wilson, 895–896.
9. This section is based on *NIVAC: Psalms, Vol. 1*, 332–358.
10. Wilson, 348.

SESSION 3

EXPRESSIONS OF DAVID'S KINGSHIP

Psalms 2, 20, 21, 45[1]

I distinctly remember the first time I was in charge of planning an overnight church retreat; just about everything seemed to go wrong. Not that others would remember it that way, because God brought things together quite apart from my plans. Looking back, I probably learned more through my failures than I would have in success; I certainly gained a new understanding of how God's strength works through weakness. God had bigger and better things in mind all along. The "royal psalms" reflect God's strength working through the failures of human kings. They were originally concerned with the human kings of Judah, uniquely authorized and empowered as Yahweh's adopted sons. But after Israel was destroyed and God's people were in exile, many of the royal psalms took on a new life of *messianic* hope and expectation. What the human kings of Israel and Judah had been unable to do, God would accomplish through his true Son, the "Anointed One," the Messiah.[2]

GOD'S ANOINTED KING REPRESENTS
GOD'S KINGDOM ON EARTH[3]

Read Psalm 2.

1. Psalms 1 and 2 together are thought to introduce the entire Psalter. How does Psalm 2 continue the theme from Psalm 1 — contrasting the righteous and the wicked? What's different about the emphasis here? Thinking about Psalm 2 as it was originally written, referring to a human king in Zion authorized to represent God's kingdom on earth, how might the psalm's message affect King David's regard for other nations?

2. The author of the book of Hebrews made the interpretive leap of equating Psalm 2:7 with the Messiah, fulfilled in Jesus (Heb. 1:5a). How does this shift in emphasis make the psalm still relevant for nations today? Read Revelation 16:13 – 14, 16; 19:19 – 21. What is the future for the kings or nations that continue to band together against the Lord's anointed king according to John's vision?

3. If we just point fingers at non-believing "nations," the psalm still fails to have much relevance for us today. However, Revelation gives us another way to look at it — the church itself has responsibility to lead God's world a certain way. Read Revelation 2:26 – 27 (which quotes Psalm 2:9). What motivation does Jesus give for aligning ourselves with God's ways rather than with the ways of those who oppose or ignore him? In what ways are

we tempted to align ourselves with the ways of the world? How can we instead act as representatives of God's kingdom on earth today?

THE LORD GIVES VICTORY TO HIS ANOINTED KING[5]

Read Psalm 20.

4. If taken out of context, Psalm 20 could easily be misconstrued as a "health and wealth gospel," where God is subject to our every whim and desire. As a royal psalm, it is concerned with the military activities of the king of ancient Israel. Read 2 Chronicles 20:1–30 for a fitting example of how this psalm may have originally been used. What are the responsibilities of the king (2 Chron. 20:3, 5, 18, 20, 27; cf. Ps. 20:1, 3)? What are the responsibilities of the people (2 Chron. 20:4, 13, 18, 22, 28; cf. Ps. 20:5, 7, 9)? How is the situation different for people living under a covenant with God compared to that of other nations (2 Chron. 20:29; cf. Ps. 20:7–8)? What is the result (2 Chron. 20:27, 30)?

5. If we fast forward to Jesus, the king who perfectly fulfills God's plans, what is the victory he was after (John 17:1–5)? What sacrifice did he offer to fulfill God's plan once and for all (Heb. 10:14)? How can we be confident that God gave him victory (Acts 2:29–36)?

GOING DEEPER

The word translated "victory" [Ps. 20:5] is the same word frequently translated elsewhere as "salvation, deliverance." On a number of occasions this Hebrew word ... clearly exceeds the sense of deliverance and achieves the more fulsome meaning of "victory." It is interesting to note, however, that the use of this particular term, "victory," rather than being a human accomplishment and potential source of pride, is always swallowed up in *divine deliverance*. To proclaim "Victory!" is to acknowledge at one and the same time that "Yahweh has delivered me."[6]

6. As God continues to build his kingdom, what are our responsibilities as people living under his new covenant? Are they different from those of the people in 2 Chronicles 20? Explain. How can we make Psalm 20 our own prayer?

GOD'S ANOINTED KING REJOICES IN GOD'S STRENGTH[7]

Read Psalm 21.

7. Based on its proximity and some common language, Psalm 21 is likely a response to Psalm 20. God's people prayed for victory (Ps. 20), and they

then celebrate the Lord's deliverance (Ps. 21). In both psalms, the desire of the king's heart is mentioned (20:4; 21:2). Seeing how those desires are granted by God (21:2), what can we assume about the desires of the anointed king's heart (see 1 Sam. 13:13–14)? How do God's answers to the king's prayer (Ps. 21:4b–6) compare to the king's request (21:4a)?

8. What were the expectations for a king in Israel (Deut. 17:14–20)? How did David's son Solomon fare according to these guidelines, just one generation after David (1 Kings 10:23–11:6)? How does this underscore the difficulties of human kingship?

9. As we look ahead to God's plan for the perfect king, how does Jesus qualify according to the expectations of Deuteronomy mentioned in the previous question (Is. 53:2–3; Matt. 1:17; Luke 9:35, 58; 22:42)? Like Solomon and others, we too still struggle with completely trusting in the Lord for continuing to deliver his people. How can Jesus help us in our struggle (Heb. 2:14–18)? How does Psalm 21 help us to anticipate great things in response to the desires of Jesus' heart (John 17)?

GOD'S ANOINTED KING
DISPLAYS KINGDOM VALUES[8]

Read Psalm 45.

10. Psalm 45 is a bit unusual, as it praises the Israelite king and his bride rather than God.[9] Taken in its original context, it was written as a wedding song for God's anointed king. What can you tell about the values in this kingdom? How are they different from other kingdoms?

11. The author of Hebrews applies Psalm 45:6–7 to Jesus in Hebrews 1:8–9. How does the description fit with Jesus' time on earth? How can it be understood looking to the future?

12. As a future bride of Christ, what preparation is necessary before the wedding (45:10–11)? What is appealing about the groom and his kingdom? How does Psalm 45 help you to celebrate Jesus as the church's future groom?

RESPONDING TO GOD'S WORD

IN YOUR GROUP:

As NIVAC author Gerald Wilson noted, the great traditional hymn "How Firm a Foundation"[10] reflects many of the thoughts found in Psalm 21,[11] and of many of the royal psalms—trusting in God, his anointed king, and his kingdom. Close your time together reflecting on the words, and singing it as a group:

How firm a foundation, ye saints of the Lord,
Is laid for your faith in His excellent word!
What more can He say than to you He hath said—
To you who for refuge to Jesus have fled?

"Fear not, I am with thee, oh, be not dismayed,
For I am thy God, and will still give thee aid;
I'll strengthen thee, help thee, and cause thee to stand,
Upheld by My gracious, omnipotent hand.

"When through the deep waters I call thee to go,
The rivers of sorrow shall not overflow;
For I will be with thee thy trouble to bless,
And sanctify to thee thy deepest distress.

"When through fiery trials thy pathway shall lie,
My grace, all-sufficient, shall be thy supply;
The flame shall not harm thee; I only design
Thy dross to consume and thy gold to refine.

"The soul that on Jesus doth lean for repose,
I will not, I will not, desert to his foes;
That soul, though all hell should endeavor to shake,
I'll never, no never, no never forsake."

ON YOUR OWN:

> *WANTED:*
> *A girl who will love,*
> *honest, true and not sour;*
> *a nice little cooing dove,*
> *and willing to work in flour.*[12]

Such was the ad for a mail-order bride in the Gold Rush era of the United States' expansion to the Western frontier. If you were to write an ad for a bride looking for a new life in God's kingdom, what would you say based on what you've learned in the royal psalms?

NOTES

1. These are known as royal psalms. Other royal psalms among Pss. 1–72 include Pss. 18, 61, and 72.
2. Wilson, 107.
3. This section is based on *NIVAC: Psalms, Vol. 1*, 106–126.
4. Wilson, 117–118.
5. This section is based on *NIVAC: Psalms, Vol. 1*, 381–395.
6. Adapted from Wilson, 385.
7. This section is based on *NIVAC: Psalms, Vol. 1*, 396–409.
8. This section is based on *NIVAC: Psalms, Vol. 1*, 699–713.
9. Wilson, 700.
10. http://library.timelesstruths.org/music/How_Firm_a_Foundation/, May 16, 2009.
11. Wilson, 409.
12. From the back cover of Chris Enss, *Hearts West: True Stories of Mail-Order Brides on the Frontier* (Guilford, Conn.: TwoDot, 2005).

SESSION 4

A CELEBRATION OF YAHWEH AS KING

Psalms 47, 48, 50, 68[1]

What is it about humans that we get so excited about being in the presence of someone important? Shaking hands with an elected official, or even a candidate; getting the autograph of someone we admire; meeting an actor or musician backstage; standing in the crowd and snapping pictures of a historic procession, whatever it might be; even visiting the birthplace of someone who's had an impact on us—and the list goes on. Maybe it has something to do with how we were made to worship—not that we always worship the right things. But there's something particularly satisfying about being in the presence of someone great. It's hard to really picture what it will be like to be in the presence of God himself, but certain psalms give us an inkling—those that celebrate God as the ultimate king. If we get a kick out of someone whose influence is here one day and gone the next, just imagine the thrill it will be to stand in the presence of the eternal God—now there's something worth telling others about!

39

ALL NATIONS WILL CELEBRATE
THE KINGSHIP OF YAHWEH[2]

Read Psalm 47.

GOING DEEPER

While it may seem obvious to the reader that "clapping the hands" is an act of joyous response, the circumstance is more complex than first imagined since the specific idiom employed here ... normally means "to strike the hands" with another individual as confirmation of a bargain or contract between parties (like a handshake).[3]

1. Just imagine what it would be like for all nations to "clap hands" together, for all to shake hands and be in agreement. Compare Psalm 47 with Genesis 11:1–9. In what respects were the nations unified in Genesis 11:3–4? How is Psalm 47 different? What brings them together (47:9; see also Rom. 4:16–17)?

2. In the original context, the image of God ascending amid shouts of joy (47:5) probably brought to mind the ark of the covenant being carried in procession to the temple, while people sang words along the lines of Psalm 24:7–10.[4] Consider Acts 2:1–12. How does this setting provide a different way to celebrate God's ascension as in Psalm 47:5? How does it represent a reversal of the events in Genesis 11:5–9?

3. In what respect does Psalm 47 describe the present reality of God's reign? In what respect does it point to hope for the future? How can God's people today participate in the unity of his kingdom and celebrate the kingship of Yahweh (Phil. 2:1–5; Gal. 3:26–28; Ps. 47:6–7)?

YAHWEH'S KINGSHIP IS FROM GENERATION TO GENERATION[5]

Read Psalm 48.

4. Psalm 48 is a "Zion Song," celebrating Mount Zion as the place on earth chosen by Yahweh as the defining point of his presence with Israel.[6] What is it about Zion that makes her so great (vv. 3, 8, 12–14)? Why do you think the kings of the earth find Zion so terrifying compared to other cities they've conquered (vv. 4–7)?

Mt Zion = "Her"

5. How did the people of Israel learn to appreciate Zion (48:2–3, 8–13)? Think of a place that's of special significance in your own story. What is it that makes it special to you? How do you pass that on to others?

6. Zion still has a special place in the hearts of Jews, Christians, and Muslims alike because of its rich history. However, many people will never visit Jerusalem, and even if they do, it is no longer the unique dwelling place of God that it was before the temple was destroyed. How can Psalm 48 help us to remember aspects of God's kingship and his faithfulness as he dwells with us now and to communicate those truths to the next generation?

GOING DEEPER

What are the Jerusalems of our own lives? Where has God erected ramparts and citadels for our protection? When have our enemies been turned back through the power of God? How can we step into the light to see and acknowledge that God is at work in our mundane lives, caring, protecting, and saving? The Old Testament narratives as a whole, and the psalms in particular, provide us with ready examples of common human beings confronted by the extraordinary presence of God in their lives. Drawing on the examples of these ancient witnesses, we may be emboldened to see God at work in our own lives [and to tell it to the next generation].[7]

YAHWEH THE KING IS JEALOUS FOR HIS PEOPLE'S HEARTS[8]

Read Psalm 50.

7. You'd think that the kingship of Yahweh would be most appreciated by his own people. But God was fully aware of the human heart and of its tendency to forget and trust in other things. Read Deuteronomy 6:3–12. What was God's primary commandment to his people in this passage? How did he expect them to remember their side of the covenant with him?

Who or what does God call on as witnesses of his people in the picture that's painted in Psalm 50:1–6?

8. God addresses people in two categories — those in 50:7–15, and those in 50:16–23. What seems to be missing in the attitude of the first group of people? What about the second group? What do they have in common (50:14–15, 23)?

GOING DEEPER

The point of offering "thank offerings" is that such sacrifices acknowledge the offerer's absolute dependence on Yahweh's grace and mercy. It is this humility and dependence that is at the core of a right understanding of sacrifice. Such humility will see sacrifice for what it really is: an outward indication of one's inner allegiance to Yahweh and obedience to his covenant commands.[9]

9. Does God rule as king in your life? The psalmist is talking to believers here, so take careful note if that's you! How do God's people today give the appearance of being obedient to God's commands, while actually rationalizing disobedience or remaining unthankful? How do people who consider themselves believers today fall in with the wicked described in 50:17–20, thinking that they somehow have God's blessing (50:21)? What needs to change?

YAHWEH IS KING OVER THE WHOLE EARTH[10]

Read Psalm 68.

10. You wouldn't want to get on the wrong side of God as he's portrayed in Psalm 68. What can his enemies expect (vv. 1–2, 11–14, 15–18, 21–23, 28–31)? How is his power put to the advantage of his own people (vv. 3–6, 7–10, 19–20, 32–35)?

11. This psalm tracks the movement of God's work in his people's lives over spans of history. What events do you get hints of in verses 7, 10, 14, and 17 that follow the history of Israel? What is the ultimate end of God's work in history (vv. 32–35)?

GOING DEEPER

The path of God's conquest in our lives ought to follow the same path: From the desert of our sin to the fruitful land of the kingdom of God, from the battles of evil within and without to the destruction of the foes and submission to God's sovereignty, from the isolation of self-concern to the communal gathering of praise in the sanctuary, God is leading his children along.[11]

12. Consider what it means for God, before whom the earth shakes and the heavens pour down (68:8), to have personal concern for the fatherless, the lonely, prisoners (68:5–6), and you. What is the potential impact of God

in your life, if you're on his side? As you look back over your own life, do you see God's progressive movement in it? Explain.

RESPONDING TO GOD'S WORD

IN YOUR GROUP:

Suppose your group was part of the procession worshipping God in Psalm 68:24–27. Describe what sort of precious tribute you would bring.

ON YOUR OWN:

In what respect are you engaged in telling the next generation about the kingship of Yahweh? It might mean communicating God's love to children or grandchildren, nieces or nephews, or it could involve interaction with anyone younger than you in the capacity of a teacher, a mentor, a youth leader, or just a friend. Think about someone this week that you would like to tell about the majesty of the King of the universe, and take the time to do it.

NOTES

1. Of Pss. 1–72, Psalm 33 also celebrates the kingship of Yahweh. More are found in Book IV of the Psalter (Pss. 90–106).
2. This section is based on *NIVAC: Psalms, Vol. 1*, 724–733.
3. Wilson, 726.
4. Wilson, 728.
5. This section is based on *NIVAC: Psalms, Vol. 1*, 734–744.
6. Wilson, 735.
7. Wilson, 743.
8. This section is based on *NIVAC: Psalms, Vol. 1*, 757–770.
9. Wilson, 763.
10. This section is based on *NIVAC: Psalms, Vol. 1*, 932–946.
11. Wilson, 946.

LAMENTING OVER DIFFICULT PEOPLE

Psalms 5, 39, 55, 56[1]

People can be so troublesome at times, can't they? It would only take a few minutes to rack up a page-long list of the times when I've been right and someone else has been wrong, and it just makes me seethe inside. The number of psalms in this category suggests it's a common frustration! Funny how reflection and prayer can change that. I distinctly remember driving home one time full of bitterness over a pretty minor issue—but it felt like an attack at the time. The black clouds in the sky matched my mood, but within moments God transformed them into a glorious day. I remember praying that God could somehow change my heart just as quickly. And he did. Instead of feeling attacked, I saw my own pride, and realized that I was actually on the same side as the person I felt attacked by. Laments take on different "flavors," but this set is particularly focused on our reaction to people opposing us. The psalmist's reaction toward enemies can be quite violent, but what I find more instructive is what is actually happening in the psalmist's heart as he turns to God for perspective and help in the midst of trying circumstances.

TIMES OF LAMENT REVEAL THE HOLY CHARACTER OF GOD[2]

Read Psalm 5.

1. The ancient Near Eastern concept of holiness outside the nation of ancient Israel focused on gods who were powerful and lived forever, but who morally shared the same human characteristics of good and evil as the people who worshipped them — anger, lust, personal gain, vengeance, manipulation, deception, to name a few.[3] How does Psalm 5 define what pleases the God of Israel (vv. 4 – 6)? How does that pose a problem for anyone in God's presence (see Ex. 33:18 – 23; Is. 6:5)?

2. How does the psalmist describe his enemies (5:9 – 10)? What seems to be their primary form of attack? How would you characterize this kind of attack (Zech. 3:1; John 8:44; Acts 5:3)? Are you exempt from such behavior (see James 3:3 – 8)? Explain.

3. Given the tendency to resemble our enemies in the destructive use of words, where does the psalmist turn for something different (5:7 – 8)? How does the psalmist focus his own word power in contrast to his enemies (vv. 1 – 3)? What is the resulting heart attitude of the psalmist compared to his enemies (vv. 11 – 12)?

GOING DEEPER

God's holiness offers sinful humanity both its greatest problem and its greatest hope. Because a holy God cannot "wink" at sin or turn a blind eye to it, sinful humans find themselves under his judgment, in need of salvation and reconciliation. But because he is also relentlessly good, he has provided a way, first through Israel and ultimately through Christ, that they can be restored to right relationship with one another and with God in order to continue to receive blessing and not judgment.[4]

TIMES OF LAMENT GIVE OPPORTUNITY FOR SELF-REFLECTION[5]

Read Psalm 39.

4. Why is the psalmist silent (v. 1)? Does his silence seem to help (vv. 2–3)? What seems to be the source of his anguish (vv. 8–11)?

5. What is the psalmist's motivation for change (vv. 12–13)? Why is it critical for him to deal with this sooner rather than later (vv. 4–6)?

6. Verse 7 stands right in the middle of the psalm. How does it become central to the psalmist's reflection? What does it teach the psalmist about his own efforts to address his sin? Can you relate to the psalmist's experience? Explain.

GOING
DEEPER

If the interior of the psalm is any indication, the irresistible message that ultimately escaped from [the psalmist's] lips was a declaration of the frailty of humans in contrast to the complete adequacy of God. His suffering was not the result of divine weakness but of human sin. Indeed, the psalmist's only hope is in Yahweh, who is both discipliner and Savior.

This true word flows out of the meditative silence that precedes, and it rightly situates the psalmist's pain in the context of sin and divine discipline. It communicates to those who surround the poet—friend and foe alike—that God is a God of both justice and salvation, who hears the prayers of those who acknowledge their sin and call on him.[6]

TIMES OF LAMENT TEACH THAT GOD ALONE PROVIDES REFUGE IN THE MIDST OF TROUBLE[7]

Read Psalm 55.

7. In a walled city, where is the enemy normally found? What about in this case (vv. 9–11)? What makes the person the psalmist is speaking against especially hard to deal with (vv. 12–14, 20–21)? Once again it seems that the words of people are most hurtful to the psalmist (vv. 3, 9–11, 20–21). Considering the history behind this relationship, why would that be particularly true?

8. What is the psalmist's initial response (vv. 4 – 8)? Does that seem realistic for the particular storm that he's dealing with? Why or why not? What alternative does the psalmist find for refuge (vv. 16 – 19, 22 – 23)?

9. What might a typical human reaction be when betrayed by a friend, especially a fellow believer? How does the psalmist respond (vv. 15 – 16, 22 – 23)? How does Jesus take this a step further (Luke 22:47 – 53; 23:33 – 34)?

GOING DEEPER

We have much to learn from the psalmist here. Often when I am attacked, I want to fight back. I want to shut the mouth of that opposing football player with a well-placed block. I want to set people straight about the true character of that rumor monger who is running me down. I want to give as good as I get, and then some. The psalmist calls out *to God* for refuge (the ability to stand up to the attacks of the enemy), rescue (deliverance from the distress and danger), and redress (setting things right).[8]

TIMES OF LAMENT SHOW THE VALUE OF GOD'S WORD OVER OTHER OPINIONS, EMOTIONS, OR COMPELLING CIRCUMSTANCES[9]

Read Psalm 56.

10. Psalm 56 certainly describes some pretty serious enemies, worth lamenting over. What do David's enemies do "all day long" (vv. 1–2, 5–6)? Twice, David asks the question, "What can mere mortals do to me?" (vv. 4, 11). How would *you* answer that question?

11. There's no doubt that David was afraid because of his enemies. That's a natural human reaction. However, he makes a deliberate choice about how to respond. What does David rely on more than his own emotions (vv. 3–4, 10–11)? How does he express his confidence in the outcome (vv. 12–13)? What would it take for you to do the same?

GOING DEEPER

[David] had every reason to be afraid. Yet trust in God's word rendered those fears obsolete.

This is a lesson I would like to learn. How does trusting in God remove fear?.... God's Word is a source of confidence to those who are beset by enemies. When we are attacked, we need to be able to draw on the stable assurance of God's Word rather than the wavering perspective of public opinion.... Too much of our faith is based on emotion and feeling. When the emotions fall—destroyed by the attacks of enemies, the misunderstanding of those around us, or our own failure of self-confidence—our sense of relationship with God can be undermined. At those moments we need to hold our emotions up to the clear testimony of God in Scripture.[10]

12. Compare what the enemy does with David's words, and their goal for David's life (vv. 5–6) with what God does with David's lament, and his goal for David's life (vv. 8, 13). How can this help in your own understanding of God's trustworthiness?

RESPONDING TO GOD'S WORD

IN YOUR GROUP:

"The testimony of the broader community of faith helps to shore up confidence. When an individual feels tempted to fall into despair, the faith of the community bears testimony to the faithfulness of Yahweh that remains eternally active."[11]

Do you find this statement to be true of the laments you have studied together? How does it help to study numerous laments at one time? How does it help to study the laments as a group of individuals? How is the corporate experience of laments different from that of an individual?

ON YOUR OWN:

Is there someone who comes to mind when you think of an enemy? When was the last time you felt like you were being attacked over something? Take some time to think about your reaction. How did your emotions play a role? Did you deal with it yourself or turn to God for help? Did you learn anything about yourself or about God? Write your own lament based on what you've learned from these psalms.

NOTES

1. Other laments in this category in Pss. 1–72 include Pss. 3, 7, 9, 10, 12, 17, 28, 30, 31, 35, 42, 43, 44, 54, 57, 58, 59, 60, 64, 69, 70, and 71.
2. This section is based on *NIVAC: Psalms, Vol. 1*, 163–175.
3. Wilson, 166.
4. Wilson, 167.
5. This section is based on *NIVAC: Psalms, Vol. 1*, 624–633.
6. Wilson, 632.
7. This section is based on *NIVAC: Psalms, Vol. 1*, 805–818.
8. Wilson, 817.
9. This section is based on *NIVAC: Psalms, Vol. 1*, 819–828.
10. Wilson, 826.
11. Wilson, 145.

LAMENTING OVER DIFFICULT TIMES

Psalms 4, 22, 40, 41[1]

People are not the only ones that can knock us down. Circumstances beyond our control also can make life miserable: illness, loss of loved ones, disasters related to the weather, unexpected financial loss, to name a few. Sometimes it's the little things that put us over the edge—unexpected things that fall apart, delay us, or just don't work out the way we had hoped. How can we remember that all these things are still in God's hands, and remain cheerful and trusting in the midst of them? How can we show the world that we have a sure hope in God that's not rocked by our circumstances? These laments help to walk us through the process, and remind us where we need to turn when difficulties besiege us, or when our own sin blinds us to the way God is at work, even when we don't see him.

LAMENTS TEACH US THAT GOD IS SUFFICIENT[2]

Read Psalm 4.

1. Psalm 4 seems to be in response to a natural calamity, such as drought that made the crops fail.[3] Where does the psalmist turn to for help (v. 1)? What indications in the psalm suggest that other people in the community are not quite so trusting (vv. 2, 4, 6a)? To what do they turn?

2. Bottom line, what do the people want from God? What is different about the psalmist's perspective (vv. 1, 6–8)? How do you see this principle worked out in other parts of Scripture (Deut. 8:1–5; John 6:26–35; Phil. 3:17–21)? What does this principle look like in people's lives today?

GOING DEEPER

The psalmist points in 4:6, when the many are described as asking "Who can show us any good?" to the seductive lure of a faith founded on pragmatism. The core of the opponents' problem is that they understand religious worship and relationship with God to be a matter of personal benefit. The focus of faith for those so inclined has a pragmatic edge: What's in it for *me*? Show me the personal benefit![4]

3. If we're honest with ourselves, we all look to things other than God at times to satisfy our needs—whether it's other people, food, work, money, status, etc. What wisdom does the psalmist offer that might help us to refocus (vv. 3–5)?

LAMENTS HELP US REMEMBER GOD WHEN IT FEELS LIKE HE'S ABSENT[5]

Read Psalm 22.

Psalm 22 is quoted by Jesus himself when he is hanging on the cross (Matt. 27:46), and it is referred to when the gospel writers describe the crucifixion (Matt. 27:35, 39, 43; John 19:23–24, 28). It's easy to understand why it is so quickly and aptly applied to Jesus. Yet, by quoting just a line of the psalm, Jesus was expecting his audience to understand its full context, and we would miss out on its implications if we simply looked at it as prophecy, pointing to Jesus' experience on the cross, rather than understanding the richness Jesus saw in the psalm as a model response to feelings of being abandoned by God.[6]

4. What is the psalmist's complaint (vv. 1–2, 6–8, 12–18)? From his point of view, how is God responding to him compared to his ancestors (vv. 4–6)? How does this fit Jesus' situation on the cross?

5. How does the oppression experienced by the psalmist serve to dehumanize both the oppressed and the oppressor (vv. 6, 12–13, 16, 20–21)? How does this go against God's intent for humanity (Gen. 1:26–31)? How does the psalmist's imagery for God counteract such dehumanizing imagery (22:9–10)?

6. Psalm 22:22 introduces a drastic change in the tone of the psalm. How is the setting different (vv. 22–23, 25)? How does the message indicate a change from the preceding verses? What is the psalmist's hope for the future (vv. 26–31)? How is this hope also reflected by Jesus on the cross?

GOING DEEPER

In the midst of despair … the psalmist finds support and hope in the worshiping community of the faithful. The enemy may dehumanize and threaten death, but in the congregation of the faithful God's righteous power is still proclaimed. When our faith is undermined by our circumstances and we are tempted to despair altogether, sometimes our only remaining hope is to place ourselves within the worshiping community of God's people. There he is praised even if we are unable to praise him. There the mighty acts of God are proclaimed even when we cannot see them. There God is present though he remains absent from our own experience.[7]

LAMENTS GIVE OPPORTUNITY TO PROCLAIM THE WORK OF GOD IN OUR LIVES[8]

Read Psalm 40.

7. The troubles described in Psalm 40 seem a bit different from many of the difficulties we've encountered in other laments, where the attack comes from the outside. What is the source of the psalmist's troubles that causes him to be trapped in the slimy, muddy pit that has no escape (v. 12)? In your own experience, how can sin get to a point where it overtakes you and causes blindness? What is the source of new sight (vv. 2–3)?

8. What is the psalmist's response to God's intervention in his life (vv. 9–10)? Do you get the sense that the psalmist is "cured" of sin (vv. 13, 17)? What impact do the psalmist's words have on others (vv. 3–4, 13–16)?

GOING DEEPER

Perhaps the primary hope the psalmist holds out for divine mercy is that while he has indeed sinned, he has not forsaken Yahweh like those who no longer "fear him." Fearing Yahweh, then, does not expect perfect sinlessness but demands a baseline loyalty and dependence on him that brings the sinner back again and again to seek God's forgiveness and blessing.[9]

9. In order for the psalmist to be honest about God's righteousness before the great assembly (v. 9), what else must he be honest about (see 1 John 1:9)? How might that be awkward for an individual, especially one in a high position such as the psalmist? What sort of attitude does it require (Ps. 40:4)? Without such honesty, what would happen to the psalmist's testimony about God (40:10)?

LAMENTS HELP US TO LOOK BEYOND OUR OWN DIFFICULTIES AND HAVE GREATER REGARD FOR THE WEAK[10]

Read Psalm 41.

10. This psalm could be referring to a time of lengthy illness at the end of David's reign (vv. 3, 5, 8).[11] If so, how does this psalm (at the end of Book I of Psalms, which is most descriptive of David's reign) compare to the confident portrayal of David as God's anointed one in Psalm 2? What implications does it have for human kingship?

11. Weakness can manifest itself in a variety of ways. What kinds of weaknesses does Psalm 41 point to (vv. 2–6)? How does David's weakness equip him to have greater regard for the weak (see 2 Cor. 1:3–5)? What alternative does he have (41:5–9)? How does the blessing for the psalmist in Psalm 41:1 compare to the blessing of the psalmist in Psalm 1?

The term [blessed] ... evokes a circumstance of "wholeness, health, prosperity, balance." The one who is [blessed] experiences life as God intended it from the beginning. This does not deny that the world in which such blessed persons move and breathe is decidedly corrupted and removed from God's original intention. But it suggests that Israel believed it was possible to experience this kind of blessed wholeness, here and now.[12]

12. Weakness is not what we expect to be honored in a kingdom. But God had even more surprises in store for his people. How does God transform our understanding of weakness in regard to his kingdom (Isa. 53:1–4, 8–9; Heb. 4:15)? What can we learn about our own role in God's kingdom in terms of how we view weakness and blessing (Matt. 5:3–12; Mark 10:42–45; 2 Cor. 12:9–10)?

RESPONDING TO GOD'S WORD

IN YOUR GROUP:

In each of these laments, the individual has some interaction with the community, whether by way of encouraging or being encouraged. Take time in your group to share how other individuals in the group have had an impact on you, and pray together, giving thanks to God for the way he is working through you corporately.

ON YOUR OWN:

What difficulties are currently besieging you or someone close to you? How can you turn one of them into an opportunity to encourage someone else to trust in God? Think about one person in particular and take time this week to make a difference in his or her life.

NOTES

1. Other laments in this category among Pss. 1–72 include Pss. 6 and 13.
2. This section is based on *NIVAC: Psalms, Vol. 1*, 149–162.
3. Wilson, 149.
4. Wilson, 160.
5. This section is based on *NIVAC: Psalms, Vol. 1*, 410–429.
6. Wilson, 424–425.
7. Wilson, 427–428.
8. This section is based on *NIVAC: Psalms, Vol. 1*, 634–648.
9. Wilson, 638.
10. This section is based on *NIVAC: Psalms, Vol. 1*, 649–663.
11. Wilson, 650.
12. Wilson, 657.

SESSION 7

PSALMS AS PENITENCE

Psalms 6, 32, 38, 51[1]

They say confession is good for the soul, but that sure doesn't make it easy! In general, our culture is neither good at confessing nor hearing confessions. Given our fierce, independent natures and our tendencies toward perfectionism, we are slow to admit our faults, and uncomfortable when we do. We would rather have superficial relationships than expose our deep-seated fears and secrets. When we hear confessions by others, we sometimes move away in fear and judgment, rather than toward them in acceptance and encouragement. Yet more often than not, when we confess before others we find that we are not alone — that many struggle with the same things we do. With confession comes release, cleansing, a burden lifted off our shoulders, and forgiveness. The psalms of penitence have much to teach us — about the results of sin, the attitude of God, and the hope for change. It is when we come to God with empty hands that we truly understand his unfailing love.

THE PENITENTIAL PSALMS ACKNOWLEDGE THE ANGUISH OF THE SOUL[2]

Read Psalm 6.

1. What can you tell about the physical and emotional state of the psalmist in this psalm? What hints suggest that there might be some guilt on his part (vv. 1, 3)?

2. What aspects of God's character does the psalmist appeal to for help (vv. 4–5)? What does the psalmist expect of God regardless of his own actions (vv. 8–10)? Do you think he's being presumptuous? Explain.

GOING DEEPER

We must realize with the psalmists that the experiences of personal pain — whether physical, emotional, or spiritual; the sense of the distance, even the absence of God in our lives; the alienation we feel from ourselves or from others; the resultant sense that we live in a hostile world — are all evidences that we live in a disordered world that is at present far less than the world God created. It is a world that in many ways defies the good intention of the creator.[3]

3. One typical response to suffering is trying to explain it away or see some good purpose in it (e.g., Rom. 8:28). How is this psalm different? How does it invite interaction with God? How can you use it to comfort yourself or others?

THE PENITENTIAL PSALMS ENCOURAGE US TO BE HONEST WITH GOD AND NOT TO HIDE FROM HIM[4]

Read Psalm 32.

4. Whether it's a light offense such as "I stole the cookies from the cookie jar" or something more serious like "I have betrayed you," what is it that causes us to want to hide our wrongdoing rather than openly confess it to someone else? According to the personal experience of the psalmist, what was the outcome of keeping silent compared to "'fessing up" (vv. 3–5)? How does the psalmist's experience relate to your own?

5. What's the difference between "the wicked" and the "godly sinner" in terms of their incriminating actions? Their attitude toward God (vv. 6–7, 9)? Their overall experience of life (vv. 1–2, 10)? What does God's forgiveness prompt the psalmist to do (v. 11)?

6. It's important not to treat too lightly either the actions of the psalmist, or those of God. What does it take to be honest with God (32:5, 6a, 9; Isa. 55:6–7)? What does it cost you? What does it take for God to forgive you (1 John 1:9)? What does it cost him (John 3:16; 2 Cor. 5:21; Heb. 9:28)? How does this psalm invite you toward an attitude of confession?

THE PENITENTIAL PSALMS DISPLAY THE DEVASTATING CONSEQUENCES OF SIN AND GUILT[5]

Read Psalm 38.

7. Sickness or debilitation does not necessarily have a direct correlation with sin, as the ancient world often assumed (see John 9:1 – 3), but in the case of Psalm 38, it does. What are the physical and emotional results of the psalmist's sin? How has it affected his relationships with other people? What hope remains for the psalmist?

8. It would be convenient if we knew that Psalm 38:1 – 17 was all pre-confession and that everything turned out for the best after the psalmist's confession in verse 18. But, like real life, the psalms aren't quite that neat and straightforward. What does it teach us about God's attitude toward sin and its consequences? Why do you suppose God comes down so harshly on sin (see Rom. 6:20 – 23)? From what we've learned in the other penitential psalms, what is our best plan of action to avoid such a situation?

9. Psalm 38 is not a template for how to treat sinners living out the consequences of their sin (vv. 11 – 12). How would you treat someone obviously suffering as a result of their sin? Suppose you were in the psalmist's shoes? What would you want friends to tell you? How would you want them to treat you? What would Jesus do (see John 8:1 – 11)?

Especially when they are made public, moments of moral failure can lead to debilitating consequences. The public today thrives on the fall of heroes, or just good men or women gone wrong. Perhaps it is a way of excusing our own failings, but we are often drawn to the scene of sinful collapse like vultures surrounding a dying animal— unwilling to depart until every recess has been revealed and every bone picked clean.

Such public outcry and continuing humiliation can lead to the destruction of useful human beings and prevents their rehabilitation.[6]

THE PENITENTIAL PSALMS SHOW THE BENEFITS OF A CONTRITE HEART[7]

Read Psalm 51.

10. The first step toward a contrite heart is being aware of your sin. If you are unfamiliar with the context of Psalm 51, read 2 Samuel 11. How does David become aware of his sin (Ps. 51 superscription; 2 Sam. 12:1–13a)? What does this teach about David's understanding of his sin (vv. 3–5)?

11. Knowing *about* our sin doesn't always equate with a willingness to confront it. What motivates David to deal with his own heart (vv. 6, 8, 10–12)?

In his expressions of self-awareness, the psalmist exhibits the kind of transparency God desires: He wants "truth in the inner parts" ... God is seeking a person whose external profession is consistent with the inner reality of his or her being that is often kept hidden away "in the entrails." ... This kind of vulnerability allows God to transform one's inner self by teaching "wisdom in the inmost place" (51:6b [NIV]). The psalmist affirms that appropriate revelation of the inner self requires divine wisdom.[8]

12. What are the benefits to David of having a contrite heart? What are the benefits to the worshipping community? How does God benefit?

RESPONDING TO GOD'S WORD

IN YOUR GROUP:

The following is a standard confession from *The Book of Common Prayer*[9] that has been passed down through the ages. How does it reflect the penitential psalms we've studied? End your group time by praying it in unison.

> *Most merciful God,*
> *we confess that we have sinned against you*
> *in thought, word, and deed,*
> *by what we have done,*
> *and by what we have left undone.*
> *We have not loved you with our whole heart;*
> *we have not loved our neighbors as ourselves.*
> *We are truly sorry and we humbly repent.*
> *For the sake of your Son Jesus Christ,*
> *have mercy on us and forgive us;*
> *that we may delight in your will,*
> *and walk in your ways,*
> *to the glory of your Name. Amen*

ON YOUR OWN:

Do you have a contrite heart? Keep a journal this week that helps you gauge your own heart—how honest you are with yourself, before God, and before other people. How aware are you of your own sin? What needs to change? How thankful are you for God's cleansing power of forgiveness? If you have trouble getting started, find a trusted friend or mentor to help you know where to begin.

NOTES

1. These are all the penitential psalms in Pss. 1–72.
2. This section is based on *NIVAC: Psalms, Vol. 1*, 176–186.
3. Wilson, 185.
4. This section is based on *NIVAC: Psalms, Vol. 1*, 543–553.
5. This section is based on *NIVAC: Psalms, Vol. 1*, 614–623.
6. Wilson, 622.
7. This section is based on *NIVAC: Psalms, Vol. 1*, 771–783.
8. Wilson, 775.
9. http://justus.anglican.org/resources/bcp/euchr2.doc, June 12, 2009

PSALMS OF CONFIDENCE

Psalms 16, 23, 27, 62[1]

As I read through the psalms of confidence, strains of numerous songs pop into my head — many contain familiar and beloved lines from these psalms that have inspired confidence in God throughout the ages. It's a wonderful thing to realize that I've inadvertently memorized God's Word through such songs — words that I can draw on when I need to shore up my confidence a bit. But even more comforting is the knowledge that others have gone before me recognizing the dangers that keep coming at us, yet finding solid ground on which to stand and face them head on. Whether we look to these psalms to put words to our own confidence, or try to build up our trust when it seems shaky, we would do well to have such songs as constant refrains in our hearts and minds.

PSALMS OF CONFIDENCE GIVE VOICE TO TRUSTING GOD THROUGHOUT THE AGES[2]

Read Psalm 16.

1. In David's time, the blessings described in Psalm 16 were very much tied to the physical land. We don't know when this psalm was written, but given the circumstances David dealt with in 1 Samuel 19–31 (when Saul was chasing him), how does this psalm express David's confidence in God? What alternative was there (Ps. 16:4)? What are the boundary lines, inheritance, and path of life David could be talking about?

2. The psalms were likely assembled in their present sequence and format during the exile, when God's people no longer had access to the physical boundary lines of their inheritance. How would the understanding of Psalm 16 shift during that time? What aspects of confidence in God would remain the same?

3. Psalm 16 is quoted twice in Acts (Acts 2:25–31; 13:35–37), understanding Jesus as the Holy One who did not see decay — in other words, he was resurrected from the grave after being there just a few days. Once again, this casts the psalm in a different light than was originally intended, yet the principle of confidence in God in the midst of even more challenging circumstances remains the same. As we look at this psalm from the perspective of people who live after Jesus' resurrection, how does it express the confidence we can have in God today (see 1 Peter 1:3–7)?

PSALMS OF CONFIDENCE HELP
US TO VISUALIZE A JOURNEY WITH GOD[3]

Read Psalm 23.

4. Psalm 23 is one of the most familiar psalms of the whole Psalter, and for good reason. What does the imagery teach about God's care of his people (vv. 1–4)? How does the desert environment of much of Israel enhance the message? Why would this have been a fitting and comforting image for David (1 Sam. 16:11)?

5. What are the risks involved in following the path of the shepherd (Ps. 23:4–5)? How do the shepherd's actions more than make up for the dangers? Let's tie this back to our reality. What are some of the risks and dangers we face in the course of following God's ways in our lives?

GOING DEEPER

Although "paths of righteousness" may have an unusual ring to our ears, it can mean no more than the "right path," that is, the one that gets you where you need to go. The ambiguity of language and context, however, allows a moral quality to creep in. If the shepherd and sheep are images of a life fully dependent and trusting on Yahweh, then "paths of righteousness" take on the meaning of a way of life that fulfills God's expectation for his follower. The sheep are not left to their own devices but are led by God himself to take the correct path—the one that gets the sheep where they need to go.[4]

6. The journey described is like a pilgrimage, an apt image for the continuing lives of Christians. What is the ultimate destination of the psalmist? The underlying assumption is that "where one is now is not where one is heading."[5] What can still change? How can the confidence of Psalm 23 help you along the way?

PSALMS OF CONFIDENCE ARE REALISTIC ABOUT DANGERS, YET SECURE IN GOD'S FAITHFULNESS[6]

Read Psalm 27.

7. Psalm 27 starts out by asking the rhetorical question, "Whom shall I fear?" (v. 1). What are some of the answers the psalmist suggests over the course of the psalm (vv. 2–3, 10–12)? Does the psalmist's confidence spring from a worry-free existence? Explain.

8. If you could boil down the psalmist's hope to one thing, what would it be (v. 4)? Does this sound "escapist" to you? How does he expand on the idea of "gaz[ing] on the beauty of the Lord and seek[ing] him in his temple" (v. 4b) in verses 8–9?

The implication of 27:8 is that the psalmist is not making an inquiry of Yahweh but is earnestly pleading for the "face" of Yahweh itself—his very presence. What he desires more than anything, requests, and pleads is for Yahweh to be present with him. Thus, the next verse continues: "Do not hide *your face* from me" (27:9).[7]

9. Psalm 27 ends with an exhortation to "be strong and take heart" (v. 14), using the same words that the Lord himself spoke to Joshua three times in Joshua 1:6–9, "Be strong and courageous." As you look throughout Israel's history, what gives the people the confidence to move ahead on God's path (Deut. 31:7–8; Josh. 1:6–9; 1 Chron. 22:11–13; 28:20; 2 Chron. 32:6–8)? How does the psalmist both exhort us and warn us to take this to heart (Ps. 27:14)?

PSALMS OF CONFIDENCE SHOW WHAT IT MEANS TO REST IN GOD ALONE[8]

Read Psalm 62.

10. Rest can be elusive to people for a great variety of reasons. Where does the psalmist find rest (62:1–2, 5–6)? How does verse 5 change the nature of the psalmist's message? How might verses 3 and 4 have something to do with the change?

11. The psalm is framed beginning, middle, and end with reasons to trust in God (vv. 1–2, 5–8, 11–12). What other influences are described that a person might trust in (vv. 9–10)? How have these other threats to trusting in God stood the test of time—are they still with us? Explain.

Frantic activity, whether in conflict with the enemy or in pursuit of wealth and personal security, does not acknowledge the strength and power of God as the place of refuge and ultimate security in the midst of trouble. Quiet repose in the face of attack is the ultimate evidence of trust in God and reliance on *his* strength.[9]

12. Rest for the soul as described in Psalm 62:1, 5 is a stillness of the whole being, a sort of "holy inactivity" in anticipation of divine action and deliverance, indicating the psalmist's trust and confidence in the Lord.[10] How do we find this kind of stillness? What challenges it?

RESPONDING TO GOD'S WORD

IN YOUR GROUP:

These psalms (16, 23, 27, 62) are all attributed to David. Make *his* psalms of confidence *your* psalms of confidence. Create a special atmosphere—burn some scented candles, lower the lights. Read through all four psalms again, out loud, pausing between each one to let the message sink in. Take time together at the end to "pour out your hearts to him," praising God for the confidence he inspires to "trust in him at all times" (Ps. 62:8).

ON YOUR OWN:

One aspect of prayer that is often neglected is trying to listen to God, not just speak to him. As you spend time in personal prayer this week, include sequences of active silence, listening for God's Spirit to speak to you. Increase that amount of time a bit each day and write down your thoughts afterward.

NOTES

1. Other psalms of confidence among Pss. 1–72 are Pss. 11, 36, 46, 56, and 63.
2. This section is based on *NIVAC: Psalms, Vol. 1*, 305–316.
3. This section is based on *NIVAC: Psalms, Vol. 1*, 430–445.
4. Wilson, 433.
5. Wilson, 442.
6. This section is based on *NIVAC: Psalms, Vol. 1*, 481–492.
7. Wilson, 489.
8. This section is based on *NIVAC: Psalms, Vol. 1*, 876–887.
9. Wilson, 884.
10. Wilson, 882.

PSALMS OF PRAISE

Psalms 8, 33, 65, 67[1]

There's something about wonderful experiences, times, or people that makes you want to share them. Why are cameras and video recorders so popular, but to record, share, and remember special moments? Why do we tend to prefer vacations with other people, or going to the movies with a friend, but to be able to share and talk about the experience? I believe praise of God falls in that category as well. When your heart is bursting with the wonders of God, they're not meant to be kept to yourself. Communal worship helps us to experience the greatness of God as well as express it together in community. As you read these psalms of praise, keep in mind the community aspect as well as the individual aspect of expressing an awe-filled sense of confidence in God's power, authority, and everlasting character displayed in this world.

PSALMS OF PRAISE RECOGNIZE GOD'S AMAZING PURPOSE FOR HUMANITY IN CREATION[2]

Read Psalm 8.

1. Like most of the psalms in this section of the Psalter, Psalm 8 is a psalm of David. Imagine him with his flocks of sheep in the desert under the clear, night sky. What aspects of the psalm flow out of an observation of creation in this setting? In the context of the vast array of the heavens, how might an individual feel in comparison? How does this psalm and other passages of Scripture reflect this feeling (Ps. 8:4; 103:15–16; Eccl. 1:4, 11)?

2. Praise for God's creation would be enough to fill a psalm. To consider that all of creation is just the work of God's *fingers*—meaning a simple task in his hands, it's just mind-boggling. But David's amazement continues. How is humanity viewed by God (Ps. 8:5–9)? How does David know this (Gen. 1:26–30; 9:1–3, 7–11)?

GOING DEEPER

The psalmist's final thought is not "How great and magnificent you are, O God, and how puny we humans are by contrast." Instead, his central insight is that in spite of the incredible chasm that separates humans and their God, so that humans appear as but minuscule specks of dust on a rock revolving around one of thousands of stars in but one of countless galaxies flung across the universe, God is still mindful of humans and has the will, purpose, and incredible gifting for our lives.[3]

3. David begins and ends the psalm praising God for the majesty of God's name (vv. 1, 9). According to Gerald Wilson, "The 'name' of God also is an extension of God himself. Where God chooses to place his name—in the land, in the temple, on his people—there God is also. The presence of his name lays claim to divine authority wherever it dwells."[4] How is God's name revealed throughout the earth (Rom. 1:19–20)? How did God entrust his name—and by extension, his presence—to his people (Ex. 3:13–15; John 1:14, 18)? What responsibility does that give us as we rule over the works of his hands (Ps. 8:6)?

PSALMS OF PRAISE REMIND US OF THE JOY OF TRUSTING IN THE LORD[5]

Read Psalm 33.

4. Following on the heels of Psalm 32:11, Psalm 33 is a jubilant celebration of Yahweh. What does the psalmist remind us about God's character (vv. 4–5)? What does he tell us about the power of God's word (vv. 6–9)? What does he reveal about God's plans (vv. 10–11)? Read over your answer again and give a shout for joy!

5. The majority of psalms in the first two books of the Psalter are laments, emphasizing the reality of hard times — specifically in David's life, but most people can relate. As you consider real-life situations, what makes it tough to "wait in hope for the LORD" (Ps. 33:20), even knowing about God's unfailing love (vv. 5, 18, 22)? What other things do people turn to instead (vv. 16–17)? What are modern-day equivalents?

Hopeful waiting — faithful endurance — rather than panicked action is the appropriate stance of God's people.... Such waiting is a sign of surrender to the power of God rather than trusting in human strength and power.... The psalms are full of exhortations and descriptions of waiting hopefully for God.... Despite suffering, struggle, and pain, Yahweh remains worthy of trust and is the only sure source of hope.[6]

6. What hints does the psalmist give that he's addressing a community of faith, not just an individual? How does a community make it easier to wait compared to being on one's own? How does a community facilitate rejoicing?

PSALMS OF PRAISE ANTICIPATE GOD'S OVERFLOWING ABUNDANCE[7]

Read Psalm 65.

7. When someone does something nice for me, I do my best to thank them. But there are times when someone goes so far overboard that I hardly know what to say—I sing their praises right and left, over and over. What phrases in Psalm 65 suggest to you this sense of abundance on God's part?

8. Compare Psalm 65 with Deuteronomy 28:1–14, written to God's people during Moses' time. What do you find similar in both passages? What's the condition for God's blessing his people in Deuteronomy 28:1–2, 9, 14? What about in Psalm 65 (v. 3)? What's different about the recipients of God's blessing in the passages?

9. If you think about the differences in Deuteronomy 28 and Psalm 65 (from question 8), what does it tell you about God's intentions and his ability to carry them out? What does it say about his "abundance" toward including people in his kingdom? How have you been a recipient of God's abundance? How can you be part of his purposes?

GOING DEEPER

The abundant display of God's care is now an evidence of his gracious mercy and forgiveness of sin. What might have been considered evidence of Israel's special status as the people chosen for divine blessing has now become an example of God's desire to draw "all flesh" [i.e., all people] (65:2) to himself to experience his salvation.... He desires nothing less than the restoration for all humanity of his original creation intention. That is reason for us to join in the party![8]

PSALMS OF PRAISE CELEBRATE GOD'S SALVATION AMONG ALL NATIONS[9]

Read Psalm 67.

10. Compare Psalm 67:1–2 with Numbers 6:22–27. What is similar about the blessing? How is it different? How does the repeated refrain (67:3, 5) emphasize the main difference?

GOING DEEPER

Often a repeated refrain drives home the main point of a psalm. In this case the main point is the hope or expectation that all the peoples of the earth will join in the praise of Israel's God.[10]

11. This psalm hints at what life will be like when all is in order again (in contrast to the disorder that has affected everything since the fall). How will God be viewed? What will be the outlook of the nations? How will the earth be affected? How are those things different from the way they are now?

12. Do you know the blessing and salvation of God? If so, how did you come to know of those blessings? How can you be part of making God's ways known among all nations? Take a moment to praise God for his ways.

RESPONDING TO GOD'S WORD

IN YOUR GROUP:

Ephesians 3:14–21 is Paul's prayer for the Ephesians. Oddly enough, it seems to capture many of the elements found in the psalms of praise we've studied in this session. That's probably because the apostle Paul was very familiar with the book of Psalms, as were the other New Testament writers. Discuss as a group what aspects of God's character Ephesians 3:14–21 captures as praiseworthy. Then agree on one single version represented by the Bibles in your group and pray the prayer from that version together.

ON YOUR OWN:

"Praise psalms contain an appeal (to self or others) to praise God, coupled with numerous descriptions of his praiseworthy name, deeds, attributes, and character. The focus is on God's role as creator, sustainer, and stabilizer of the universe—humanity's sole assurance of continued stability and reliability in a chaotic world."[11]

In your own experience, what attributes of God have you seen or deeds has he done to make him praiseworthy? Keep a running list during the week. Take some time to praise God yourself, and share what you've thought about with at least one other person.

NOTES

1. One other psalm of praise among Pss. 1–72 is Ps. 29.
2. This section is based on *NIVAC: Psalms, Vol. 1*, 198–220.
3. Wilson, 205.
4. Wilson, 200.
5. This section is based on *NIVAC: Psalms, Vol. 1*, 554–564.
6. Wilson, 561–562.
7. This section is based on *NIVAC: Psalms, Vol. 1*, 904–913.
8. Wilson, 909.
9. This section is based on *NIVAC: Psalms, Vol. 1*, 925–931.
10. Wilson, 927.
11. Wilson, 65.

LITURGICAL PSALMS

Psalms 15, 24, 26, 66[1]

For some, liturgy brings to mind the idea of mindless repetition. How unfortunate that preparation to meet God in worship could ever be considered monotonous! The Israelites took worship seriously. Worship consisted of more than praise — it was recognition of the sinful nature, repentance, petition for divine deliverance from suffering, and thanksgiving for God's faithfulness. God's people prepared the body, mind, and spirit any time they came into the presence of their holy God, taking stock of their lives and the consequences of their decisions. These liturgical psalms include elements of the ritual practices used to prepare the hearts of worshippers as they approached the temple. Though we rightly rejoice in the freedom of meeting God anywhere today, we should be challenged to consider what it means to prepare our hearts before God anytime we meet him in our daily lives.

LITURGICAL PSALMS TEACH US HOW TO EXAMINE OUR HEARTS BEFORE ENTERING GOD'S PRESENCE[2]

Read Psalm 15.

1. As you read through the list of requirements for living in God's presence, what is your initial reaction as to whether or not you qualify? How does Paul's description of human righteousness in Romans 3:10–18 compare? What is God's solution for bringing together unholy people with a holy God (Rom. 5:6–11)?

2. If the Israelites understood these requirements as sinless perfection, no one would have ever been allowed in the temple. However, the Hebrew word used (*tamim*) points to "a way of life that is 'whole' by virtue of consistent dedication to the 'way of the LORD.' Those so dedicated will be judged as having fulfilled the demands of 'righteousness.' "[3] Given this understanding, how does Psalm 15 invite examination of the heart prior to entering God's presence? If we understand God's presence to be available to us at all times, not restricted to the temple in Jerusalem as it was during David's time, what implications does it have for when we should reflect on our attitudes toward God and neighbor?

GOING DEEPER

The one who is ready to enter God's presence is *not* the one who has taken the prescribed ritual precautions or who knows how to adopt the requisite outer attitudes of worship. Instead, the one who lives a life of transparency, where one's inner thought is reflected truly in speech and deed — such a one is ready to meet God. The kind of worship envisioned here breaks out of the confines of temple and Sabbath to infect the rest of the week and all of life. It is aware of God's presence day by day and not just at prescribed moments of worship. Here life becomes a form of worship in which ordinary human activities and relationships are invested with uncommon sacramental character.[4]

3. Psalm 15:2 – 5 isn't an exhaustive list of sin, but sure gets at a lot of key interactions with others. If you look at them as couplets, there are six categories of interactions to think about. What are they? Which do you struggle with the most? If you deal with them on a regular basis — that is, if you live a way of life that invites dependence on God to correct them, what does the psalmist describe as the outcome (v. 5b)?

LITURGICAL PSALMS HELP US TO UNDERSTAND WHO WE ARE IN RELATION TO GOD[5]

Read Psalm 24.

4. Psalm 24 begins with God's ownership of the world and everything in it. On what is his authority based (v. 2)? How does the psalmist view God's role in the world (vv. 7 – 10)? What do you imagine it would be like for David to write this psalm as the king of Israel?

GOING DEEPER

The psalmist is pointing beyond God's dominating authority to his essential role in the very origin of the world and its continued existence. What he is saying is not that we are Yahweh's world because he has taken it for his own by power of conquest, but that the world must acknowledge its absolute dependence for being, sustenance, and continued existence on its creator and sustainer — Yahweh alone. There is no other alternative, since there is no independent existence apart from Yahweh.[6]

5. The questions posed in verse 3 are similar to Psalm 15:1, but the context of God's kingly reign paints a slightly different picture — like subjects approaching their king's throne for mercy. What are the requirements for receiving blessing from the king (24:4 – 5)? How does this further strengthen the picture of our dependence on God alone?

6. The scene shifts in verse 7. Having gained admission into God's temple, his worshippers joyfully await the arrival of God himself. Imagine a large group of people responding in this question-answer format, exalting the glory of God. How would the claims of Psalm 24 encourage anticipation and hope? If you as a community are facing a threat, how can it help put things in perspective?

LITURGICAL PSALMS INVITE GOD'S PENETRATING GAZE ON OUR HEARTS[7]

Read Psalm 26.

7. When first reading this psalm, it seems like it must be about Jesus to be true, or else the psalmist is very arrogant and misguided to make such claims. But keep in mind the comments on Psalm 15 (question 2), where a blameless life is not characterized by sinless perfection, but rather a way of life that continually depends on God's mercy and grace. Compare 26:4–5 with Psalm 1:1. What steps is the psalmist taking to live the life of the faithful? What other actions point to a life depending on God (26:1b–3, 6–8)?

GOING DEEPER

Clearly the foundation of the psalmist's hope and security is not personal integrity and sinlessness but Yahweh's fierce loyalty and enduring faithfulness, which provide a way for essentially sinful humans—who acknowledge their complete dependence on Yahweh's mercy and grace—to continue to walk in his presence.[8]

8. The psalmist claims that he has trusted in the Lord without faltering (literally "I will not wobble"[9]), and that his feet stand on level ground (vv. 1, 12), yet he pleads with God for vindication, redemption, and mercy (vv. 1, 11), rather than losing his soul in the way of sinners. Is this a contradiction in terms? How does this fit with the reality of the Christian life in your experience?

9. In 26:2, the psalmist invites the Lord to test and try him, to examine his heart and mind. Given what we've reestablished as the blameless life, what do you think the Lord will find? How quick are you to invite God's penetrating look at your heart? What will he find? Why is this an appropriate action to take at the altar (v. 6)? What wonderful deeds might result for the psalmist to proclaim aloud (v. 7)?

LITURGICAL PSALMS INVITE THE COMMUNITY OF FAITH TO PRAISE GOD FOR HIS FAITHFULNESS[10]

Read Psalm 66.

GOING DEEPER

According to the response to the first question of the Shorter Westminster Catechism, the chief end of man is "to glorify God, and to enjoy him forever." Psalm 66 takes almost the same position when it calls "all the earth" to "sing the glory of his name; make his praise glorious!" (66:2).... I do think this statement captures in its essence the nature of human responsibility in this life and on this earth. We are in our deeds, words, thoughts, and relationships to "glorify God" — in other words, to make his glory known to the cosmos.[11]

10. What are the deeds of God that are remembered by the faithful in verses 3–7? What deeds in your own life or faithful community do you remember?

11. Not everything God does in our lives seems immediately praiseworthy at the time. How does the psalmist turn times of difficulty into praise (vv. 8 – 15)? How does that help you to praise God in times of suffering as well as abundance?

12. How does the psalmist glorify God through his final testimony (vv. 16 – 20)? How does it challenge your own personal relationship with God?

RESPONDING TO GOD'S WORD

IN YOUR GROUP:

As you end this study of Psalms, take time as a group to remember God's "fierce loyalty" and "enduring faithfulness." What have you learned about him, or what deeds has he accomplished in your life during the course of your study? Praise him together in prayer.

ON YOUR OWN:

As you enter your own church sanctuary this week to worship, be sure to prepare your heart. Read Psalm 15 and think about all aspects of your life as you enter into the presence of the living God. Confess anything that might stand between you and God, and ask his forgiveness so that you may worship with true joy.

NOTES

1. In a sense, all psalms can be used liturgically, but these are the only psalms in Pss. 1–72 that make specific reference to the ritual practices of Israelite worship. More appear in later psalms.
2. This section is based on *NIVAC: Psalms, Vol. 1*, 296–304.
3. Wilson, 298.
4. Wilson, 303–304.
5. This section is based on *NIVAC: Psalms, Vol. 1*, 446–458.
6. Wilson, 455.
7. This section is based on *NIVAC: Psalms, Vol. 1*, 470–480.
8. Wilson, 473.
9. Wilson, 472.
10. This section is based on *NIVAC: Psalms, Vol. 1*, 914–924.
11. Wilson, 922.

LEADER'S NOTES

SESSION 1 LEADER'S NOTES

1. The law of the Lord sometimes refers to the first five books of the Bible, but more generally, it's God's Word in its entirety, which would include the entire Bible (including Psalms). It should be a delight that people want to meditate on continually, not a burdensome set of rules and regulations, or boring obligation. To meditate on God's Word continually requires reading it, thinking about it, experiencing it daily — essentially to make it a way of life, not just something we refer to from time to time. It should include the Bible in its entirety, not picking and choosing the parts we prefer.

2. The righteous way is fruitful and full of life, watched over by God himself. It is a life based on trust in the Lord that draws deeply on his provision, so that when circumstances are difficult there are no fears. The water imagery fits well with the river of the water of life flowing from the throne of God and the Lamb, pointing to Jesus as the very source of life that is described in Psalm 1.

3. The wicked are like chaff that blows away in the wind. Any accomplishments, any status, any rationalizations for why life was lived a certain way will be destroyed in the final judgment. It will be a waste of a life, regardless of the effort that was put into it. Jesus associated with all kinds of people considered wicked, but called them to change their lives. Interestingly, he was most harsh with those who were associated with God's law — pointing out how they failed to live out its true intent. We all need to examine our lives on a daily basis — too often we tread too close to the line in living our lives according to our own plans, not God's.

4. The heavens declare the glory of God, that is, his ability to create, sustain, provide, protect, and even to destroy creation. Think of the effects of rain, tides, warmth, light, storms, gravitational pull—what magnitude, power, balance, and beauty! Day and night from the beginning of creation the story has been the same, reaching all of humanity, regardless of culture, language, or geography. The sun is personified as joyfully doing what God created it to do, having a great impact on all of human habitation in a way that cannot be ignored.

5. God gave us his law to warn us from ways we could harm ourselves, and to guide us according to the best way to live, resulting in great reward. His law is perfect, trustworthy, right, radiant, pure, sure, precious, sweet, and righteous. When we follow his law, it refreshes the soul, makes us wise, and gives joy to the heart and light to our eyes.

6. As the psalmist points out in verse 12, we tend to be blind to our own errors. We need God's Word, "sharper than any double-edged sword, . . . dividing soul and spirit, . . . judg[ing] the thoughts and attitudes of the heart" (Heb. 4:12) to reveal our sin—both the unintentional and the willful kind. We need God's help to guide us, and even more than that, we need to fix our eyes on Jesus—who willingly and joyfully ran his own course—trusting in his forgiveness and following in his footsteps, to find the joy that God intends for us.

7. Because the arrangement of lines stands out quite clearly in Hebrew, the acrostic structure is a glaring clue that it's a psalm associated with attaining wisdom. It's also a helpful tool for remembering each element of the psalm. The vocabulary also points to its intent to instruct—the psalmist repeatedly turns to God for instruction, demonstrating a humble attitude and desire to learn. Other vocabulary frequently used in wisdom psalms (though less so in Psalm 25) is vocabulary such as "Blessed are those . . ." or "the fear of the LORD."

8. The psalmist is very honest, humbly acknowledging both past sin and ongoing struggles with sin. He has troubles from his enemies, but equally difficult are the troubles from his own rebellious ways. In his petition before God, he doesn't attempt to hide his sin but seeks God's mercy, love, and forgiveness—this is the imperfect heart that God wants us to reveal to him.

9. God is trustworthy; he won't allow those who belong to him to be shamed. According to the covenant promise God has made, he is loving and merciful, forgiving sins. He teaches those who will humbly listen to his ways, and he draws near to them when they are lonely or troubled. The psalmist paints a very personal picture of his relationship with God, built on a foundation of trust and grace. Hopefully, studying these psalms will cause us to want us to grow closer to God in similar ways.

10. There may be a footnote in your Bible pointing out that this is another acrostic poem, like Psalm 25. It's longer by virtue of the fact that each Hebrew letter introduces four lines. Like Psalm 1, there is a clear contrast between the wicked and the righteous, and as we learned from Psalm 19, the righteous life is ultimately more beneficial. The problem, however, is that the benefits of righteousness aren't too obvious in this life — evil men seem to be prospering despite the teaching that they will suffer harm.

11. You don't get the sense that the psalm is looking at life with rose-tinted glasses. It describes the reality that things are not right in this world — the evil prosper and the righteous suffer, at least in the short run. David certainly had his share of dealing with unjust men throughout his life and reign over Israel. The wisdom that he shares is not just head knowledge, but based on long-term observations and experience.

12. Over and over again the psalmist affirms that the righteous get the better end of the bargain in the end, and even great benefit now. The inheritance of the righteous is eternal, while the benefits of the wicked come and go like grass — not even lasting a whole lifetime in many cases. There's no comparison — despite present appearances; God remains in control and rules justly.

SESSION 2 LEADER'S NOTES

1. Psalm 52 shows the contrast between the evil man, specifically Doeg the Edomite, and the righteous man, David. The evil man will suffer consequences for his actions — he will be snatched up and torn from his tent, uprooted from the land of the living. In contrast, the righteous man will flourish like an olive tree in the house of God — similar to the picture painted in Psalm 1.

2. Doeg the Edomite is a flesh-and-blood example of evil rather than some hypothetical example of unrighteousness. He's eager to earn Saul's approval and doesn't care about the lives of the priests or their families. For David, that's a problem in regard to the massacre Doeg carries out against those who helped David. But more than that, it's an offense against God's kingdom as Doeg aligns himself with Saul, a man who has abandoned God's agenda for his own, and whom God has rejected as his righteous king.

3. Although Doeg, Saul, and David all share some responsibility for the death of the priests and their town, God clearly orchestrated the events to accomplish his purposes as prophesied many years earlier.[1] Although David may have had Doeg in mind as he wrote of evil men, it applies to anyone who boasts of the achievements of evil rather than trusting in God. It suggests that David's psalms, though specific to his situations, also apply to other circumstances more generally. It is an encouragement to all of us to put our hope in God alone — only then can we flourish under God's unfailing love rather than be uprooted.

4. Those with David assume Saul is the enemy, and that God has given David this opportunity to be rid of him (1 Sam. 24:4). However, David is clearly less concerned with his own safety than with honoring God. By showing compassion and respect to Saul, David (at least temporarily) challenges Saul's definition of David as an enemy (1 Sam. 24:19). He is confident that God will accomplish his purposes regardless of whatever danger it poses, so that David will live to ascend the throne as prophesied.

5. In verses 3 and 10, David declares God's love and faithfulness, reaching to heaven itself. In verses 5 and 11, David exclaims, "Be exalted, O God, above the heavens; let your glory be over all the earth." Clearly he understands God's love and faithfulness as he takes refuge in him despite trying and threatening circumstances. He glorifies God's ways as he lives the life

of a chosen child of God (see Col. 3:12–17). He extends that same love to Saul, who rules as God's anointed, as he protects him and pursues peace as far as it is in his power.

6. When God saves people through faith, he saves them for a purpose—he has prepared good works for them to do (Eph. 2:8–10) and equips his people to accomplish them (Eph. 4:11–13). Whatever we do according to that purpose gives glory to God. Be specific as you think about what God has called you to. Our personal safety is not part of the bargain. God provides refuge for us in the midst of our circumstances, not necessarily escape from them. How we treat "enemies" could very well be part of the purpose he has in mind for us (see Matt. 5:43–48).

7. The psalmist describes a longing for God that involves his whole being—body and "soul" (vv. 5, 8, NIV). It suggests a time in the psalmist's life when he can't find God to satisfy his desires. Jesus uses this same picture of living water when talking to the Samaritan woman at the well, and soon after that, at the Festival of Tabernacles—using the understanding of thirst to point to longings that can only be fully satisfied through trust in God.

8. David experienced God in the sanctuary (63:2), and was helped by God in the past (63:7–8), so he understands what he's missing. He clings to the memory of God's presence, confident that he will experience God again, despite current circumstances. Jesus knows the Father's presence even better, as the exact representation of God's being, having been with him since before Creation, and intimately knowing him even while on earth. But even Jesus experienced separation from God on the cross, where he thirsted—body and soul—because he willingly took on humanity's sin.

9. According to Ephesians 6:12, our enemy is not flesh and blood, but Satan himself. Although Jesus defeated him on the cross, the father of lies still has limited reign on earth, doing his best to isolate us from those who remind us of God's help. Making Psalm 63 our own is like putting on the armor of Ephesians 6:13–20, reminding us of God's love, standing firm even when that love seems distant, living in faith until the time we will never again thirst (Rev. 22:1, 17).

10. In the end, David is nowhere near the battle where Saul dies. The psalmist's account is describing the heavenly battle that is going on, as if the curtain is pulled back for us to see the spiritual realm that is normally

invisible. The account in 1 Samuel is describing the details of the actual earthly battle. Although it's about the same event, it's the equivalent of what's going on "on stage" as well as "behind the scenes."

11. David's situation was desperate—his enemy overpowered him, and without God's intervention he would have died. But God was responsive to his cries for help because he delighted in him. God is faithful to those he has called, and who are faithful to his ways. Nothing can stop his plans. When we are on God's side—watch out world!

12. God equipped David in tangible ways—strengthening his arms and feet, and working providentially through circumstances to encourage David and discourage his enemies. In the 1 Samuel account, God uses the Philistines and specifically keeps David *out* of the battle so as not to be directly involved in killing Saul or his sons. Think about ways God has tangibly helped *you* in times of crisis, both in equipping you and working providentially through people and circumstances.

NOTE

1. Bill T. Arnold, *The NIV Application Commentary: 1 & 2 Samuel* (Grand Rapids: Zondervan, 2003), 313–316.

SESSION 3 LEADER'S NOTES

1. The nations feel constrained by God's ways — they would rather do things their own way (similar to the wicked of Psalm 1) — so they conspire against him by conspiring against his anointed king. But like those in Psalm 1, they are warned — they will be destroyed. They are no match for God, who sits in heaven and laughs — only the righteous will prosper. While Psalm 1 emphasizes the individual, Psalm 2 speaks of nations and their rulers. From King David's point of view, he has a responsibility to represent God's kingdom on earth, which means in that historical context expanding his territory and subduing the nations opposing Israel.

2. The struggle between worldly nations and God's ways continues today. Any nation or ruler that sets itself against God will eventually be judged for its actions. Revelation portrays a picture very similar to the one in Psalm 2:1–3, where the nations conspire together to destroy God's forces, but as in Psalm 2, the result is laughable — God easily destroys them.

3. Faithfulness is rewarded with victory over those who oppose God. But to be sure we ourselves are not opposing God, our actions and choices must reflect God's kingdom values now. Instead of putting ourselves first, we must think of others. We must live differently, humbly depending on God's mercy, and pointing others toward "the freedom and glory of the children of God" (Rom. 8:21).

4. The king leads his people by bringing them together to pray, fast, offer sacrifices, and seek God's help. Then he leads them confidently into battle, relying on God rather than his own power. Following victory, the king leads the people in praise of God. The people are continually called to trust in their God and king, and to worship God. Unlike the other nations, they live under the protection of God's covenant with them. They are called to trust in him rather than human strength, resulting in miraculous victory, joy, and peace.

5. Jesus came to earth to bring eternal life to people. He sacrificed his own life, even when Israel abandoned him, failing to follow him in seeking the Lord. His one, perfect sacrifice was sufficient for all people, eternally. The fact that he rose from the dead is proof of his victory over sin and the completion of God's plan for humanity.

6. Like the people of 2 Chronicles 20, we are called to trust and worship our God and king—not to trust in our own strength. Today, that means answering the call of our king, Jesus, and going out in his name to advance his kingdom, praising God for the victories he accomplishes in people's lives. As we consider the desires of Jesus' heart (John 17:2–3), that others would receive eternal life by knowing the only true God, we can address Psalm 20 as a prayer for the continued work of Jesus' Spirit, with confidence of the peace and joy he will bring to us and others.

7. God chose David to replace Saul as king because David was a man after God's own heart. That's not to say that all his desires were pure—they clearly were not. But God's anointed king is expected to align himself with God's revealed purposes; otherwise his prayers will not be answered. The king asks for life, and God grants him eternal life, eternal blessings, splendor, majesty, and the joy of God's presence. God answers in much greater abundance, beyond what the king has requested.

8. The Israelite king was to be chosen by God and was to be a native Israelite. He was not to accumulate horses, wives, or gold, and he was to know and follow God's law. Solomon's accumulation of horses and chariots, wives, and gold, and his seduction to follow the gods of his wives was a big problem in God's eyes. His many "marriages" were political alliances with the other nations that his father, David, had fought against. The story of Solomon emphasizes the conflict within human leaders who are supposed to point people to trusting in God, but are themselves trusting in other things.

9. Jesus was chosen by God; he was an Israelite descended from David; he came from humble beginnings; he remained humble; and most of all, he remained in God's will, not giving in to any temptations. He is perfectly qualified to be God's anointed king, yet also relates to our struggle having been human himself. David asked for life (Ps. 21:4); Jesus asked God for *our* lives, and we can anticipate God's answer in great abundance based on Psalm 21. Jesus' resurrection from the grave secured not only his own life, but the lives of all who put their faith in him.

10. Victory is important in this kingdom, but it is based on God's blessing (45:2), in order to promote truth, humility, and justice (45:4). Justice is all-important, since it reflects God's standard (45:6). Only someone who loves

righteousness and hates wickedness is qualified to be king (45:7). There is also a concern for succession to the throne (45:16). Most kings are more concerned with their own power, glory, and self-interest, at the expense of their own people and other nations. God's kingdom represents a drastic departure from the norm.

11. Jesus certainly displayed all the values portrayed in this psalm, from lips anointed with grace, to the furtherance of justice, truth, humility, and righteousness. But his majesty was hidden, except when he was glorified at the transfiguration (Matt. 17:2). When Jesus returned to heaven, his full majesty was restored. It is fitting to understand him as the groom, waiting for his bride, the church, when the great wedding feast of heaven occurs (Rev. 19:7).

12. The bride must put her family behind her, and honor her new lord. To be part of a nation which honors truth, humility, righteousness, and justice, and to be married to the most excellent of men clothed in splendor and majesty, has got to have great appeal! Likewise, we must put behind worldly values and honor the ways of Jesus. The bride is marrying someone enthralled by her beauty; she is honored and decked in splendor herself, as we will be dressed in fine linen, bright and clean, displaying our righteous acts (Rev. 19:8). The psalm is one of celebratory joy and gladness that helps us anticipate the marriage of the church to Jesus, the most excellent of men.

SESSION 4 LEADER'S NOTES

1. In Genesis 11, the whole world spoke the same language and agreed to build a city out of bricks to make a name for itself. As a result, God scattered the people over the face of the whole earth and confused their language. Conversely, in Psalm 47 they are all coming together in unity to praise God, not themselves. They come together as the people of Abraham, which, Romans tells us, is a unity according to faith in God, through grace—not something we earn or are born into.

2. We're told in Acts 2:5 that all nations were represented at Pentecost. Through God's gift of the Holy Spirit, they were all praising God together, everyone understanding each other despite their scattered languages. It is a picture of God bringing all nations together to praise him (as in Psalm 47)—a reversal of what he did at the Tower of Babel—and celebrating Jesus' ascension amid shouts of joy that it was impossible for death to keep its hold on him (Acts 2:24).

3. As Psalm 47 states twice (vv. 2b, 7), God *is* the great King of all the earth. He is *already* seated on his holy throne, ruling over the nations (v. 8), and this because he is the Creator. There is nothing the nations can do to frustrate God's plan. But this plan has clearly not been fully realized—there is still distrust, suspicion, prejudice, anger, and hatred between individuals and nations. But the psalm points to a time when that will be fully true—it is a sure hope. In the meantime, Christians are called to imitate Christ and live as citizens of God's kingdom, valuing others and worshipping God; Psalm 47 gives a text through which to do that.

4. God himself is Zion's fortress (48:3). He makes Zion secure (48:8). It is his guidance, over and above the physical structure, that gives the psalmist confidence (48:14). Similarly, it is God who causes the other forces to flee in terror. Zion was no doubt a significant city to tackle, but God has a history of defending his people, as well as the ability to bring fear to the heart through natural forces arrayed against his enemies (48:6–7).

5. Zion was a beautiful city (v. 2). It had a history as a reliable fortress (v. 3). The testimony of God's faithfulness that was passed on from generation to generation was shown to be true over time (v. 8). The temple in Zion encouraged meditation on God's unfailing love (v. 9). God had a reputation throughout Judah and to the ends of the earth (vv. 10–11). Walking

around Zion caused her people to remember what God had done, and pass the stories on to the next generation (vv. 12–13). In our own experiences, some places are spectacular because of their particular features, but more often, a place is special because of the memories attached to it. We pass that on through visits, testimonies, pictures, etc.—especially to our children.

6. For most of us today, the physical location of Jerusalem (or any other city) is less important than the significant milestones God has placed in our lives, particularly related to a relationship with him. We should become adept at having a ready testimony for who and what we believe (see 1 Peter 3:15), making visible to others what stands as a foundation in our hearts.

7. "Love the LORD your God with all your heart and with all your soul and with all your strength" (Deut. 6:5). Knowing their tendency to forget, God warns his people to keep his commandments continually before them—in their hearts, teaching their children, talking about them wherever they go, making tangible reminders that will help jog their memories—particularly when they are flourishing and start to take God for granted. The picture painted in Psalm 50 is a court scene, with God as the judge and the heavens and earth as witnesses, where God's people are judged regarding their covenant obligations.

8. The first group of people is identified as "my people" and "Israel" (v. 7)—obedient on the surface, they are making the right kinds of sacrifices and offerings. But they seem to lack hearts of love and thankfulness for God. They seem to think God needs their offerings, confusing who is dependent on whom. The second group more blatantly disregards God's laws, acting like the wicked (v. 16), though they claim to be part of the covenant. They're on a slippery slope heading toward destruction. Neither group acknowledges God with thankful, submissive hearts—failing to show their utter dependence on him as their mighty king.

9. It's very easy to get caught up in the routine of appearing religious while missing the heart of worshipping God, even if it looks different today than when this psalm was written. Many use prayers, routines, sacrifices, and service to try to bargain with God, even if subconsciously—it can be very subtle. A quick read of the Sermon on the Mount (Matt. 5–7) is a great reminder of how we fail to heed God's instruction as he intended it when

we read the specifics of Psalm 50:17–20. None of us is righteous on our own (Rom. 3:10), but we need an attitude of humility, confession, and thankfulness—utter dependence on the mercy and salvation of our God and king—to stand before the God of justice.

10. It's effortless for God to scatter his enemies. He needs no help from his people to utterly crush them. Some of the imagery may be a bit violent for modern tastes, but in the day it was written, it communicated in ancient conventional language God's absolute power over other nations and their gods.[1] They will be scattered, or brought to humble submission, and will bring God tribute themselves. His own people rejoice. Not only does he protect them from their enemies, he takes care of the most needy, makes their land fruitful, and bears their burdens on a daily basis. The Lord is their strength and their salvation.

11. The Israelites were led by God out of Egypt, through the wilderness, then into the Promised Land. There they settled as God drove out the original inhabitants. Then God established his sanctuary at Mount Zion, in Jerusalem. Ultimately, all kingdoms will come to worship him, proclaiming God as Lord of all the nations.

12. It is simply amazing that the God of the universe is the same God who counts the hairs on your head (Matt. 10:30), and cares about every detail of your life. The potential for his work in each person's life is incredible. Take time to consider both where you have come from and what God might have in store for you.

NOTE

1. Wilson, 943.

SESSION 5 LEADER'S NOTES

1. God's holiness is defined by his character which is good through and through; evil is incompatible with his presence. God hates wrong and destroys anything wicked in his presence, including evil people, arrogance, and lies. This is a problem for any human, as exemplified by Moses and Isaiah. Human beings are by nature sinful, and even those who are his children cannot stand in God's presence without him making some sort of provision for them.

2. The psalmist's enemies can't be trusted; they're full of malice and intrigue; they tell lies; they rebel against God. What's described shows how powerful destructive words can be against another person. Satan is also described as an accuser, a liar, a murderer, and a deceiver. We are all prone to such activity. As James describes it, the tongue is a restless evil that can't be tamed, full of deadly poison.

3. The psalmist is dependent on God's love and mercy to come into God's presence. Only by relying on God can he go the "straight way." Instead of responding in kind to his enemies, the psalmist cries out to God desperately for help. As a result, the psalmist experiences the joy of being in God's presence, in contrast to his enemies whose hearts are filled with malice.

4. The psalmist is silent in order to keep himself from sinning, particularly in the presence of the wicked. But his silence only increases his anguish. His trouble comes from his own sin, which God is punishing him for.

5. The psalmist feels a distance from God — he feels like a stranger in God's presence. At the same time, he has come to recognize how fleeting and futile life really is; if he doesn't resolve his relationship with God, it could be too late, and his life is nothing apart from God.

6. Verse 7 indicates a shift in the psalmist's thinking. He acknowledges his sin and his utter dependence on God for any hope of meaning in his life. His own attempts to change things through his silence were useless — his heart continued to burn without God's help to cleanse and restore him.

7. Normally, you would expect to find an enemy outside a walled city. In this case, the enemy is within — prowling about on its walls, never leaving its streets. It's a close friend, a fellow Israelite who has betrayed the psalmist. On the surface he remains a friend, but underneath he is at war with the

psalmist. Because there was a relationship of trust and fellowship before, the enemy would be uniquely armed to hurt his friend with words, by betraying knowledge of his former friend.

8. The psalmist responds in anguish, fear, trembling, and horror. He wishes he could flee and find refuge elsewhere, like a dove finding safety in the desert. That might provide temporary relief, but is probably not realistic for an ongoing situation where he must coexist with his enemy/former friend. Instead the psalmist finds refuge in God in the midst of his circumstances. While the battle rages around him continually, day in and day out, he is sustained by God.

9. Typically, we lash out in some way when we've been hurt — whether we talk about the person who's betrayed us behind their backs, or try to get back more directly. The psalmist leaves it in God's hands. His thoughts are certainly harsh — wishing his enemies would go down alive to the grave (55:15), but he trusts God to carry out whatever punishment is appropriate. Jesus, who was betrayed by all humanity, shows love and forgiveness in the face of hatred. Even to those closest to him, Judas included, Jesus speaks with mercy and grace to the very end.

10. David's enemies are in hot pursuit; they press their attack all day long. They twist his words and scheme over his ruin. They conspire, lurk, and watch his steps, hoping to take his life. People can do plenty of harm! Physical, mental, and emotional harm of all kinds can destroy a person — by taking his or her life, destroying the confidence to move forward in life, or ruining a reputation.

11. David trusts God and relies on his word. According to that word, he has confidence that God will deliver him from death and keep his feet from stumbling, so he gives God thanks. In order for us to act similarly, we have to first *know* God and his Word, and then act on it. Not an easy task when you begin to think of real situations and how you respond to them.

12. Whereas David's enemies are twisting his words and plotting to harm him, God is recording David's tears on his scroll, or as some translations say, preserving his tears in his wineskin — they are precious to him. In addition, God has delivered David from death, allowing him to walk before God in the light of life — he is paving the way for life in abundance for David. It seems obvious that we should trust in someone who loves us so

much, and has our best interests in mind, yet we are sometimes hard to convince. As we experience God's faithfulness, and understand his Word more clearly, hopefully our trust in God will grow.

SESSION 6 LEADER'S NOTES

1. The psalmist turns to God for help and seems quite confident that God will respond favorably. Other people seem to be angry at God. They don't see God responding to their needs, so they seek help elsewhere — probably offering sacrifices to the false gods of neighboring countries.

2. People are very me-centered, looking to God for fulfillment, but quickly turning to other sources when he doesn't meet their expectations. The psalmist looks for relief as well, but has a deeper understanding of God's provision — his very presence, and the peace and joy that come from trusting in him. This is a theme throughout Scripture — seen clearly when God's people wandered in the wilderness; during Jesus' time when people focused on healings and feedings; and addressed by Paul, who emphasized the difference between immediate gratification and God's glory. People have not changed. Even in a church context, we can be overly focused on how God will provide for *me* or *my* church, and ignore the bigger perspective of what it means to be in relationship with him.

3. Verse 3 points to a greater knowledge of God and his relationship with his people. Verse 4 reflects heartfelt thought, listening to God, and repenting. It requires intentional time spent with God away from others. Verse 5 points to action that follows greater understanding. God wants us to trust him and live out our lives sacrificially (see Rom. 12:1–2).

4. Despite the psalmist's cries to God, there's no response — he feels abandoned, unsure why God is silent when he is suffering. His enemies mock and attack him, with no end in sight — he's likely to die. The psalmist is aware of God's faithfulness to his ancestors, but from his perspective, he's in a worse situation and is getting less response. Jesus experienced greater suffering and mocking at the hands of his enemies than anyone else. He who was closer to God than anyone had ever been, felt God's abandonment and silence more greatly than anyone else ever could.

5. The psalmist describes himself as a worm, the most insignificant, even destructive creature on earth. His enemies are compared to bulls, roaring lions, and dogs — fierce animals who have no mercy for their prey. Unlike the creatures who were made in God's image and given a special role in God's creation, they have been reduced to the status of beasts by their actions and separation from God. By contrast, God is described like

a midwife, present from birth, helping the psalmist in such a way that his life is totally dependent on him. Such interaction with God restores a sense of dignity to humanity.

6. Instead of crying out on his own, the psalmist is with his worshipping community. There, in the midst of other believers, he is able to proclaim God's faithfulness even though he is still suffering. His hope in God seems to be restored. The psalmist is able to look ahead and see God answering his cries, restoring humanity to its proper place in creation, and satisfying rich and poor alike, while God's praise is proclaimed throughout the world and to all generations. As Jesus quotes this psalm, he no doubt understands the depth of misery of being abandoned by God for a time, but also looks ahead to the promise of being restored to God, and bringing many with him (Heb. 2:10).

7. It is the psalmist's own sin that overwhelms him. It is as if he is drowning in quicksand with no hope for change until God forcibly lifts him out and sets his feet on firm ground. Sin by its very nature is deceptive. One false step makes the next false step easier, while we convince ourselves of our righteousness. Pretty soon we can be trapped in a web of sin that is hard to get out of, and even to see clearly. Light exposes darkness. It is God himself who gives us new sight to see ourselves as we are, and to sing a new song.

8. The psalmist sings God's praises before the great assembly. The psalm suggests that he is honest about his sin and clear about God's intervention—his love and mercy—which saves the psalmist from the troubles he gets himself in (and the trouble he will get into again and again). He has a humble recognition of his tendency toward sin. But his honesty allows some to see and fear God and put their trust in him. Others will be ashamed over their actions taken against the psalmist.

9. In these circumstances, it's impossible to proclaim God's righteousness without the psalmist also confessing his own sin—no doubt a potential source of public embarrassment. It requires an attitude of humility and trust in God rather than pride or concern over the opinions of other people. But without such honesty, the psalmist would rob God of an opportunity to proclaim God's great faithfulness, salvation, love, and truth to others. As far as a contemporary application, when confessing *specific* sins that have injured others, it is usually best to confess only to those who already

know about the sin involved. In sensitive situations, one should consult a pastor.

10. If this is describing David, it would seem on the surface that something went wrong in God's plan. The human king is very vulnerable — sadly lacking compared to the king God installed on his holy hill (Ps. 2:6). It emphasizes the frailty of human kings and the superior nature of Jesus as an eternal king, of whom David was only a lesser type.

11. Weaknesses described in Psalm 41 include vulnerability to enemies, illness, sin, death, lack of an heir to carry on a name, and slander. Because David himself experiences weakness, he is better able to have compassion and help others in his kingdom. Alternatively, he could act like his enemies and take advantage of the weaknesses of others. The difference is similar to the contrast of the blessed and the wicked in Psalm 1, where one is walking according to God's ways and the other is not.

12. God took everyone by surprise when his Messiah came in the form of the Suffering Servant. No one expected the eternal king to come in weakness. But God's kingdom is unlike the world. As we walk in Jesus' steps, we have a completely different view of weakness. God's power is made perfect in our weakness, so we can experience blessing just as we are, regardless of circumstances. In addition, we can have greater respect, compassion, and comfort for those around us who are weak, following the model Christ established for us.

SESSION 7 LEADER'S NOTES

1. The psalmist is faint; his bones are in agony; his soul is in anguish. He is exhausted from weeping. This psalm does not present a clear confession of guilt, but the fact that he expects God's rebuke and discipline suggests some admission of guilt, particularly since God seems so far from him. The ancient world often saw a direct connection between guilt and illness, so the psalmist's difficulties might be viewed as divine punishment.[1]

2. The psalmist appeals to God's unfailing love (*hesed*), a word that in Hebrew defines the essence of God's enduring faithfulness, mercy, and kindness according to his covenant promise to love his people. He also appeals to the glory due to God's name—the psalmist will be worth more alive than dead because living he can praise God's name. He knows that God has heard his weeping and cry for mercy, and that his prayer is accepted. He's also confident that his enemies will be put to shame. The psalmist knows God well enough to know this is consistent with his nature—without necessarily knowing how things will turn out for himself.

3. Rather than give a lot of explanations or conclusions, the psalmist simply recognizes his difficulties, and God's acknowledgment of his pain. By appealing to God's unfailing love, it teaches us what it means to turn to our compassionate God in time of trouble, even if we're somehow at fault. When we're in pain, we don't always need answers, but someone who understands. The psalm shows us how we can find comfort by turning to God, and also how to follow in God's footsteps, being compassionate listeners ourselves.

4. Beginning in the garden of Eden, there's always been a tendency to want to hide or cover up sin. Partly due to guilt and shame, and partly due to fear of consequences, everyone struggles with the inclination to hide sin rather than confess it. For the psalmist, silence was much worse than confession. His guilt remained; he felt God's disapproval; and he suffered physically. As soon as he confessed to God, he experienced the freedom of forgiveness and loss of guilt. People might have varied experiences, but in general, guilt has a way of continuing to eat away at people until it's resolved.

5. Both the wicked and the godly sinner do wrong. It's their response toward God that's different. The godly sinner seeks God after doing wrong. Like a mule or a horse, the wicked continue to oppose God, sometimes with no

moral understanding of what they're doing, and certainly no inclination to change. As a result of God's forgiveness, the godly sinner is blessed, surrounded by God's unfailing love. The problems of the wicked are compounded. The forgiven psalmist sings for joy!

6. We must have a humble attitude that truly admits when we're wrong without trying to blame someone else or rationalize, and seek out God's help from the bottom of our hearts. Our pride might be hurt; we might have to face certain consequences; moving forward, we must change our ways (which can be hard). But the true cost is borne by God who had to punish his own Son, Jesus, in order to pardon us. For justice to be served, someone has to pay the price — and God chose to do so out of love. The short-term cost of our confession is greatly outweighed by the benefits of forgiveness. We should truly "rejoice in the LORD and be glad" (Ps. 32:11).

7. Physically, there is no health in his body — his bones and back are in pain, his wounds are festering, his eyesight is failing — it sounds like he is about to die. Emotionally, he is overwhelmed by guilt, depressed, and isolated, withdrawing from interaction with other people because he is so overcome by his anguish. His friends and neighbors avoid him and his opponents take advantage of him. His one remaining hope is God, the only one who can save him.

8. God is serious about sin. It has devastating consequences on all aspects of our lives — physically, emotionally, socially — which lead to death. His desire is for us to live according to his ways, leading to eternal life with him. His heavy hand is meant to turn us to him in repentance from sin before we face eternal consequences. As we weigh the consequences of sin, it should urge us all the more to live godly lives — not achieving sinlessness, but turning from habitual sin and turning regularly to God in repentance and trusting in his unfailing love and mercy.

9. Sadly, we often *do* act like the false friends described in Psalm 38:11. We should have the attitude of reformer and martyr John Branford, who, watching a prisoner going to his death, said, "There, but for the grace of God, goes John Branford."[2] It is in times like these that we can have the greatest effect on friends, both in ministering to their physical needs, and speaking the truth in love, encouraging them to turn to God for help and

change their ways. As Jesus ministered to the woman caught in adultery, he showed mercy and encouraged a radical transformation of her life.

10. David obviously knew what he did to Bathsheba and her husband Uriah, but was in denial of his sin until Nathan confronted him with a parable. Then he saw his sin in a much bigger context—his sin was against God, not just individuals, and it fit a larger pattern of sin from the day he was conceived until the present.

11. David's heart change is God-prompted. He is aware of God's desire for change in his "secret, inmost place," and he misses the joy of God's presence as a result of his sin. God's disapproval has come in the form of "bone-crushing" discomfort, prompting David to seek God's cleansing power.

12. David experiences God's mercy and compassion, and is restored in relationship to God with a clean heart, giving him joy and gladness. The whole community benefits when their king is right with God, as they corporately worship and come to understand more clearly the importance of a broken, contrite heart. In addition, they benefit from the strengthened understanding of God's code of laws and the importance he places on maintaining them. God is pleased to be in relationship with his people once again, receives their praise and offerings, and continues to build his reputation as loving and merciful but just.

NOTES

1. Wilson, 178.
2. http://en.wikipedia.org/wiki/John_Bradford, June 12, 2009.

SESSION 8 LEADER'S NOTES

1. David was well acquainted with enemies and the prospect of losing his royal inheritance, but he trusted God for everything — refuge, blessing, joy, his path of life. Though many chased after other gods, David clearly understood the uselessness of such pursuits — they would only increase sorrows. David was probably allotted a small portion of land since he was the youngest in his family. Yet God made him king of Israel, an inheritance and path of life that had great responsibility, but also great blessing and honor.

2. The message becomes more spiritualized when not tied directly to the land. Although the Israelites don't experience the blessings of the land, they rejoice in God himself being with them. The challenges of enemies, dangers, and lures of other gods remain the same, though the details are different from David's time. How much more do God's promises mean to exiles, who cling to the hope of returning to the Promised Land, and who must remain content with "the lot" in life God has assigned them in the meantime! Because God continues to guide and instruct, and remain at his people's right hand, they remain unshaken (16:7 – 8).

3. In one regard, the message is the same. We face circumstances that challenge us both physically and spiritually, yet our hope is in God — apart from him we have no good thing (16:2). He is with us; he instructs us; he protects us. But Jesus also "make[s] known to [us] the path of life" (16:11) in ways that those who lived before Jesus could never know. He has established a new path for us that involves new birth leading to an eternal inheritance that can never perish, spoil, or fade (1 Peter 1:3 – 4), though for awhile we still face trials of many kinds. We can be confident that God is with us now and in the future.

4. As a young man David was a shepherd. The shepherd is the provider, protector, and guide for his sheep. The psalm points to the loving-kindness of the Lord as a shepherd over his people. The sheep lack nothing because the Lord is their Shepherd. Even in a place where resources are scarce, God can provide abundantly and knows exactly what his people need. As a shepherd himself, David was very familiar with what was required to take care of creatures who were dependent on him, and who would quickly wander to their deaths without his guidance and care. He was both aware

and capable of dealing with dangers, and knew where he had to go with his sheep. The connections to God caring for his people are very transparent.

5. The shepherd must take his sheep through treacherous valleys, and the rod and staff are reminders of dangers to be avoided (such as beasts and cliffs). The scene shifts in verse 5, but enemies are ever-present. Yet the psalmist has no fears because of the shepherd's capable hands to guide and protect. Some of the dangers we face are from without — difficult circumstances, people who give us a hard time, etc. But following God holds other challenges as well — to grow in character, step out in faith, avoid temptations. These too can be dangerous pitfalls on the journey.

6. The ultimate destination is life with God himself (which is no longer linked to a specific geographical place). It is a lifelong journey in which we need to grow in faith and maturity, learning to let go of our own plans and trusting God's paths of righteousness — he guides us to the good stuff. You'd hope we would want this, but sheep are not known for wise decision-making! The psalmist paints a picture of the benefits of trusting God for his provision, protection, and guidance, which should help our own confidence. But we can be grateful that the shepherd doesn't just let his sheep decide what's best.

7. In 27:2 – 3, the descriptions of the psalmist's enemies are progressively worse — the wicked advance, enemies and foes attack, an army besieges, and war breaks out against him. In 27:10 – 12 there is more of an emphasis on betrayal — his father and mother forsake him, oppressors lead him astray, and false witnesses rise up against him. It would seem that the psalmist has every reason to be anxious, being attacked from all sides, yet his trust in God wins out hands down.

8. The psalmist says there's only one thing he seeks — to dwell in the house of the Lord all the days of his life and gaze on his beauty as he seeks him in the temple. Yet he doesn't seem to be escaping so much as reenergizing in God's presence in the midst of his enemies. He repeatedly asks to see God's face; he seems obsessed with knowing God's presence.

9. "Be strong and courageous" are words of encouragement used by Moses, Joshua, David, and Hezekiah, all in conjunction with the promise that God will be with them and never forsake them in accomplishing his purposes. It is God's presence on which the hope of Israel rests. The psalmist

encourages us to have confidence in the Lord, but also warns us to wait on him, not taking things into our own hands as we face challenges.

10. The psalmist finds rest in God alone. Because God is such a rock, the psalmist can't be shaken—he knows God will save him. Yet in verse 5 it is as if the psalmist has to remind himself again of that truth, as if he lost some sense of that rest. In between, the psalmist complains of his enemies, who sound like bullies. Perhaps their assault causes him to have to remind himself of God's salvation.

11. Verse 9 describes the influence other people have on us. That could be a function of their status (lowborn/highborn) and our pursuit of power and control, or simply the degree to which we care about people's opinions. But the psalmist reminds us that they don't amount to anything (even though they still have great influence over us). The trust we put in riches is described in verse 10—regardless of how we attain them (or long for them). This, too, remains a powerful influence that competes with people's trust in God today.

12. "Artur Weiser offers a powerful translation of the opening phrase: 'My soul is still if focused on God alone.' With eyes on the storm, there seems no hope to overcome it. With eyes turned toward self, there is no personal power equal to the task. Only when one is able to focus on God alone does the power of the storm recede in response to his command, 'Peace! Be still!' Only then is our lack of power swallowed up in his complete adequacy."[1]

NOTE

1. Wilson, 886.

SESSION 9 LEADER'S NOTES

1. Psalm 8 portrays a great appreciation for God's creation—heaven and earth and all the creatures that fill it—and for God as the Creator of it all. In particular, the heavens—moon and stars reflecting the beauty of the night sky—give rise to appreciation of God's majesty. In considering such a vast array, it's easy to be humbled, feeling like a speck in the midst of it all, insignificant in comparison to the eternal Creator who put everything in its place, while human beings come and go in this world like grass that quickly withers.

2. Humankind is made in God's image and is given a special place of glory and honor—just a little lower than the heavenly beings. Though creatures ourselves, we have been given the responsibility to care for and govern the creation in which God has placed us. God made this clear in the story of creation, and reiterated it with Noah, making a covenant with all creation.

3. God reveals his majesty in his creation; his eternal power and divine nature can clearly be seen in the heavens and earth. But he is also a God who desires to be known, so he revealed himself more clearly to his people by giving his name to Moses, and then most clearly through sending his Son Jesus, the exact representation of his being (Heb. 1:3). Knowing God helps us to better understand his purposes and carry out his desires on this earth. We have great responsibility as God's ambassadors to bear his image in a way that reflects him well.

4. God speaks truthfully; he is faithful and just; his love is unfailing. Simply by his word, God has the power to create and sustain the heavens and the earth. God's plans are guaranteed—no one can thwart his purposes; rather, he foils plans that don't line up with his.

5. It really comes down to trust. For all the characteristics we know about God, it is often tempting to rely on more tangible, immediate solutions than wait on him. Individually, we rely on ourselves, our education, money, status, etc. Psalm 33:16–17 describes what a nation relies on for strength—its military might. Corporately things have not changed much, even if horses have been left behind.

6. In 33:1–3, the righteous are encouraged to praise God on numerous instruments, definitely a community setting. In verse 12, the whole nation is addressed rather than individuals. And the pronouns used in

verses 20–22 are plural (*we, our, us*), again pointing to a community of faith. It's much easier to give in to temptation when you're on your own. The community can encourage one another and become stronger than its individual parts, reminding one another of God's faithfulness through word and song, rejoicing together at the many ways God demonstrates his unfailing love.

7. Verse by verse speaks of God's abundance. *All people* come in response to God (65:2). Despite *overwhelming* sin, God forgives (65:3). We are *filled* with the good things of God's house (65:4). God answers with *awesome* deeds of righteousness (65:5). He is the hope of *all the ends of the earth and farthest seas* (65:5). The *whole earth* is filled with awe at his *wonders* (65:8). God enriches the land *abundantly* (65:9). Streams are *filled*; furrows are *drenched*; carts, grasslands, and meadows *overflow with abundance* (65:9–13). There's a sense in which everything God touches is filled or overflowing with his abundance, singing for joy as a result.

8. Both passages describe the kind of abundant blessing that God desires to bestow on his people. But blessing was dependent on obedience, and God's people were not obedient — in fact they were overwhelmed by sins. Blessing was only possible because of God's forgiveness. In Deuteronomy 28, the recipients of blessing were limited to God's holy people, the ancient Israelites, who would demonstrate God's blessings to the other nations. But in Psalm 65, the net has widened — all people will come (v. 2); those God has chosen has expanded to the ends of the earth (v. 5).

9. God's desire is to bless people, but our disobedience was an issue from the very beginning. However, God's plans to bless people were never thwarted. He had a plan from the start for dealing with sin, which became progressively clearer as time went on — first through the sacrificial system and ultimately through Jesus. His desire is to be inclusive of as many as will come to his kingdom. Anyone who belongs to God's family is a recipient of his abundant forgiveness, since we have all been overwhelmed by sin. His abundant blessings begin now, but will be realized completely when his kingdom is fully established on earth. We can take part in God's purposes as we join in praise of him, and participate in sharing his good news and hope to the ends of the earth.

10. The language used in Psalm 67 is very reminiscent of Numbers 6, except that in Numbers the blessing was directed exclusively toward the Israelites, while in Psalm 67 it extends to all peoples, causing them in turn to praise God. The refrain, emphasizing "all the peoples," further underlines the focus on the nations compared to the Israelites.

11. God's ways — his salvation, justice, guidance, and blessings — will be known and praised by all peoples. The nations will be glad and sing for joy as they learn to depend on God. The land will be fruitful as God created it to be. The picture painted is a world in harmony with God and with one another, a very different world from what now exists.

12. The majority of Christians today have benefited greatly from the spreading of God's Word to the nations beyond the Israelites. As a result we know his ways and can be glad and sing for joy. Letting others know of God's salvation should be a natural outpouring of the joy God has given us, but too often we keep it to ourselves. May we all grow in the joy of sharing God's ways with others!

SESSION 10 LEADER'S NOTES

1. If we're honest with ourselves, even those who think of themselves as "basically good people" would have a hard time meeting this list of requirements. Jesus alone qualifies. Paul's list in Romans 3 addresses just about the same characteristics as Psalm 15, and affirms wholeheartedly that all people fall short of the mark. But thanks be to God! Because of his love, God made allowance for ungodly, unholy people like us, by allowing Jesus to take on any and all punishment we deserve so that we might be reconciled to God.

2. Psalm 15 provides specific criteria, particularly focused on our interactions with other people, that help us to think about how we have fallen short of God's standards. It invites confession, repentance, and reconciliation prior to coming into the presence of God, similar to Jesus' instruction in Matthew 5:23–26. This should be a daily attitude toward God and others, not something we do when we "go to worship" once a week. Our lives should be characterized by worship.

3. The first characteristic underlies all the others — living a righteous life encompassing thoughts, words, and deeds. Then there's our speech, treating our neighbor well, keeping company with the faithful rather than evildoers, being true to our word, and having integrity with our finances. Everyone struggles in different ways, but if you didn't find something in this list that hits home, you're not thinking deeply enough. As we pursue life the way God wants us to, we are told we will never be shaken — good news indeed.

4. God's authority in the world comes from creating and sustaining it. Nothing would even have its existence apart from God. God is described as a glorious, invincible king, who is strong and mighty. From King David's perspective, it seems like it would be rather humbling to honor such a king who is above you. It creates a bit of a tension from a human perspective, but also keeps humanity in line — intended to rule temporarily, keeping God's world in order as God ordained.

5. To receive God's blessing, we must have clean hands (i.e., not hands that do wrong) and a pure heart. In addition we must not trust in anything but God. God wants us entirely dependent on him, not fooling ourselves into thinking that anything else can provide life or protection.

6. Psalm 24 serves as a reminder of how strong and mighty God is. Whatever the community is facing, God—the creator and sustainer of the world—can handle it. As king of the whole earth and its inhabitants, he will protect and provide for those belonging to him, regardless of how bad it is. Therefore, welcoming God into the midst of the community is a source of hope, celebration, and anticipation of better days to come.

7. The psalmist is aligning himself with the righteous people of God rather than people who are deceitful, hypocritical, evildoers, or wicked, along the guidelines of Psalm 1:1. That's not to say that he doesn't reach out to such people (after all, Jesus did!), but he doesn't follow their lifestyle. In addition, the psalmist trusts in the Lord (26:1b); he is completely transparent before God (26:2); he relies on God's love and faithfulness (26:3); he experiences God's cleansing forgiveness (26:6); he tells others about God's work in his life (26:7); and he loves being in God's presence (26:8).

8. The Christian life is characterized by battle, not simply victory. Although God has given us victory over sin, we remain in a world where temptation and struggle are the norm as God purifies us. If we portray ourselves as finished products, free of sin, we deceive ourselves and others. An honest picture of a Christian is one of humble confession, living on God's grace, rather than someone who is somehow better than others by virtue of faith.

9. As in any normal human being, God will no doubt find sinful thoughts, words, and deeds. What is striking is not the psalmist's sin, but his transparency. Many of us are prone to try to cover up sin, even though we know God sees all. By allowing God to examine his heart, the psalmist also invites God's forgiveness, appropriate at the altar, and worthy of proclaiming aloud.

10. In general, God keeps nations in check. More specifically, the psalmist refers to the crossing of the Red Sea in 66:6, where God led the Israelites to freedom beyond the expectations of anyone involved. As we look back in our own history, either as individuals, communities, or nations, we should see numerous ways God has turned the tide in the favor of his people. We should take time to notice and remember such deeds.

11. The psalmist interprets times of suffering from God's perspective. God keeps our feet from slipping. He brings on hard times to test our faith, letting us see it for what it is. He brings us through times of trouble, showing

us how he answers our prayers. The psalmist portrays real life where suffering is normal, yet shows God's purposes and faithfulness so that we can continue on in hope, praising God even before we know his answers to our prayers.

12. The psalmist testifies to his personal relationship with God in the midst of life and suffering. He is convinced of God's love, of his prayer being heard, as long as he is not running the other way, cherishing sin instead of God. The psalmist is an encouragement to our own prayer lives, challenging us to examine our hearts as we pray, and calling us to tell others about God's love.

Psalms Volume 1

Gerald H. Wilson

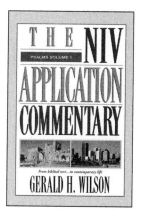

Most Bible commentaries take us on a one-way trip from our world to the world of the Bible. But they leave us there, assuming that we can somehow make the return journey on our own. They focus on the original meaning of the passage but don't discuss its contemporary application. The information they offer is valuable—but the job is only half done!

The NIV Application Commentary Series helps bring both halves of the interpretive task together. This unique, award-winning series shows readers how to bring an ancient message into our postmodern context. It explains not only what the Bible meant but also how it speaks powerfully today.

Perhaps more clearly than any other part of the biblical canon, the Psalms are human words directed to God. Yet, through the Holy Spirit, these honest, sometimes brutal words return to us as the Word of God. Their agonies and exaltations reflect more than the human condition in which they were created; they become the source of divine guidance, challenge, confrontation, and comfort. However, it is possible to misapply them. How can we use the Psalms in a way that faithfully connects God's meaning in them and his intentions for them with our circumstances today?

Drawing on over twenty years of study in the book of Psalms, Dr. Gerald H. Wilson answers these questions and reveals the links between the Bible and our present times. Wilson opens our eyes to ageless truths for our twenty-first-century lives.

Available in stores and online!

Share Your Thoughts

With the Author: Your comments will be forwarded to the author when you send them to *zauthor@zondervan.com*.

With Zondervan: Submit your review of this book by writing to *zreview@zondervan.com*.

Free Online Resources at
www.zondervan.com

Zondervan AuthorTracker: Be notified whenever your favorite authors publish new books, go on tour, or post an update about what's happening in their lives at www.zondervan.com/authortracker.

Daily Bible Verses and Devotions: Enrich your life with daily Bible verses or devotions that help you start every morning focused on God. Visit www.zondervan.com/newsletters.

Free Email Publications: Sign up for newsletters on Christian living, academic resources, church ministry, fiction, children's resources, and more. Visit www.zondervan.com/newsletters.

Zondervan Bible Search: Find and compare Bible passages in a variety of translations at www.zondervanbiblesearch.com.

Other Benefits: Register yourself to receive online benefits like coupons and special offers, or to participate in research.